Praise for
Greater

"Writes Steven Furtick, '*Good enough* leaves you stuck in stagnation. Grasping for *greatness* leads to endless frustration. But *greater* is a third way.' My advice? Don't waste another second to embrace the third way. In *Greater,* Steven shows you that God's vision for your life is ready to be ignited. Go ahead—strike the match!"

> —JENTEZEN FRANKLIN, senior pastor of Free Chapel,
> Gainesville, GA, and *New York Times* best-selling
> author of *Fasting*

"If you ever felt like you were meant for more yet have settled for less in life, then Steven Furtick's new book, *Greater,* is for you! Its proven biblical insights and practical applications will put you on your path to the greater life."

> —KERRY SHOOK, senior pastor of Woodlands Church,
> Houston, TX, and coauthor of the *New York Times*
> best-selling *One Month to Live* and the national bestseller
> *Love at Last Sight*

"Most people crave more out of life and sense there is a greater reason for our existence. Pastor Steven's new book, *Greater,* is the perfect book to stir your faith, build your spiritual confidence, and inspire you toward the unique calling for your life. If you read only one book this year, make it *Greater.*"

> —CRAIG GROESCHEL, senior pastor of LifeChurch.tv,
> Oklahoma City, OK, and author of *Soul Detox*
> and *Dare to Drop the Pose*

"My friend Steven Furtick has an insatiable passion for the church to discover the fullness of life in Christ. In *Sun Stand Still,* Steven dared us to pray audacious prayers and believe God for the impossible. Now in *Greater*, he walks us through what it looks like to live out an audacious life—a life marked by nothing less than greatness God's way!"

—JOHN BEVERE, best-selling author of *Relentless* and *The Bait of Satan*

"Steven Furtick boldly pursues God with audacious faith like no one else I know. He is unapologetic about allowing God to accomplish greater things through him. This book will inspire you to do the same. To reach for greater. To believe for greater. To be greater."

—STOVALL WEEMS, lead pastor of Celebration Church, Jacksonville, FL

"In every generation God empowers a few great leaders to speak his truth with boldness. Steven Furtick is one of those voices in our generation. In his new book *Greater*, you will learn how to embrace God's present plan for your greater calling and purpose."

—CHRISTINE CAINE, director of Equip and Empower and founder of the A21 Campaign

"*Greater* is about walking in God's higher purpose for your life. Whether that's as a teacher, preacher, leader, parent, musician, artist, engineer, or entrepreneur, Steven Furtick will show you how to let go of your fears and embrace your greater purpose in God."

—ISRAEL HOUGHTON, Grammy Award–winning recording artist and worship leader of Lakewood Church, Houston, TX

"People today are bored, depressed, and confused because they have settled for 'good enough.' But 'good enough' is keeping us from living the life that God has called us to. In *Greater*, Steven

Furtick embarks on a brilliant journey of transformation that every follower of Christ needs to take. This book delivers!"

—PERRY NOBLE, senior pastor of NewSpring Church, Anderson, SC, and blogger on leadership, vision, and creativity

"Pastor Steven's powerful yet vulnerable teaching grabbed my heart, equipped my mind, and stirred my soul like no other book I've ever read. This is one I will return to again and again. For anyone who has ever dared to dream but doesn't know how to turn their dreams into reality, *Greater* is a must-read."

—LYSA TERKEURST, *New York Times* best-selling author of *Made to Crave* and president of Proverbs 31 Ministries

"Some of us wear ourselves out trying to achieve 'greatness.' Others of us miss our calling and settle for 'good enough.' In *Greater,* Steven Furtick shows us the surefooted path to the *Greater* life."

—MARK BATTERSON, lead pastor of National Community Church, Washington, DC, and author of *Primal* and *In a Pit with a Lion on a Snowy Day*

"Steven Furtick is living exactly what he's written about in this book—start small, dream big, and see what God will do! Our church has been massively blessed by the example of Pastor Steven, his family, and Elevation Church. Take it from the best. Don't underestimate what God can do with your small start. Get this book and be encouraged!"

—DINO RIZZO, lead pastor of Healing Place Church, Baton Rouge, LA, and author of *Servolution*

"Steven Furtick understands spiritual vision like few people I know. If you desire a life beyond your imagination, read this book! *Greater* will take you to a whole new level and invite you to experience the power of God every day."

—JACK GRAHAM, senior pastor of Prestonwood Baptist
Church, Dallas, TX, and author of *Powering Up*

"The distance between desire and doing is often intimidating because we don't know where to begin. But in *Greater,* Steven Furtick shows that God's 'greater' for our lives is as far away as our first step of obedience."

—ED YOUNG, senior pastor of Fellowship Church, Dallas,
TX, and author of *Outrageous, Contagious Joy*

"Steven Furtick is in my head again with *Greater.* He's challenging me to be greater—and the good news is that all I have to do is think big and start small."

—TIM SANDERS, author of *Today We Are Rich* and CEO
of Net Minds

"My friend Steven Furtick calls us to a faith-filled life of trusting and believing God for greater lives than the ones we are living now. It's not about us, though. It's about God's greater glory in and through our lives. If you are ready for a life-altering experience with Jesus Christ, pick up a copy of *Greater.*"

—JAMES MACDONALD, senior pastor of Harvest Bible Chapel,
Chicago, IL, and author of *Always True* and *10 Choices*

DREAM BIGGER.
START SMALLER.
IGNITE GOD'S VISION
FOR YOUR LIFE.

GREATER

STEVEN
FURTICK

MULTNOMAH
BOOKS

GREATER
PUBLISHED BY MULTNOMAH BOOKS
12265 Oracle Boulevard, Suite 200
Colorado Springs, Colorado 80921

All Scripture quotations, unless otherwise indicated, are taken from the Holy Bible, New International Version®, NIV®. Copyright © 1973, 1978, 1984 by Biblica Inc.™ Used by permission of Zondervan. All rights reserved worldwide. www.zondervan.com. Scripture quotations marked (NKJV) are taken from the New King James Version®. Copyright © 1982 by Thomas Nelson Inc. Used by permission. All rights reserved.

Italics in Scripture quotations reflect the author's added emphasis.

The Culpepper story in chapter 10 is taken from Raymond F. Culpepper, *No Church Left Behind: Every Church Can Be G.R.E.A.T.!* (Cleveland, TN: Pathway, 2007). Used by permission.

Details in some anecdotes and stories have been changed to protect the identities of the persons involved.

ISBN 978-1-60142-325-2
ISBN 978-1-60142-326-9 (electronic)

Cover design by Ryan Hollingsworth

Published in the United States by WaterBrook Multnomah, an imprint of the Crown Publishing Group, a division of Random House Inc., New York.

MULTNOMAH and its mountain colophon are registered trademarks of Random House Inc.

Library of Congress Cataloging-in-Publication Data
Furtick, Steven.
    Greater : dream bigger, start smaller, ignite God's vision for your life / Steven Furtick.
— 1st ed.
        p. cm.
    ISBN 978-1-60142-325-2 — ISBN 978-1-60142-326-9 (electronic)
    1. Christian life. 2. Elisha (Biblical prophet) I. Title.
    BV4501.3.F875 2012
    248.4—dc23
                            2012012830

Printed in the United States of America
2012—First Edition

10 9 8 7 6 5 4 3 2 1

SPECIAL SALES
Most WaterBrook Multnomah books are available at special quantity discounts when purchased in bulk by corporations, organizations, and special-interest groups. Custom imprinting or excerpting can also be done to fit special needs. For information, please e-mail SpecialMarkets@WaterBrookMultnomah.com or call 1-800-603-7051.

I dedicate this book to the LTrain.

The start you were handed wasn't much,
but you worked what you had.
And God made your life into something much greater
than anyone could have reasonably expected.
Thank you for teaching me to hunt
and giving me a tractor-trailer to learn punk rock.
I'm proud to be your son.

Contents

Steve and Me

I used to want to do great things for God. That was before I found something greater.

> > >

My mom says she'll always remember that she was sitting in a social studies class when the loudspeaker beeped and crackled and someone announced that President John F. Kennedy had been shot. All the kids would be going home for the day.

I wonder if I'll always remember that my two sons and I had just shared kung pao shrimp at P.F. Chang's when I stopped in my tracks on the way out the door. I had to make sure I had correctly read the words that were scrolling across every television within sight:

Apple founder Steve Jobs—dead at 56.

I can't explain why, but my hands were shaky and sweaty as I pulled my iPhone out of my pocket to verify.

One of the first things I saw was a statement from President Obama. He said that Steve Jobs "was among the greatest of American innovators." That "he transformed our lives, redefined entire industries, and achieved one of the rarest feats in human history: he changed the way each of us sees the world."

Then I looked at my Twitter time line to see what the rest of the world was saying about Jobs. Everybody seemed to be weighing in. The outpouring was overwhelming.

"R.I.P. Steve Jobs. You led the world into the 21st century."

"R.I.P. Steve Jobs. You improved life as we know it."

"Steve Jobs—On behalf of every dreamer sitting in his or her garage who is crazy enough to try to change the world, you will be missed."

I suddenly felt the urge to tweet my own thoughts about his passing. But it felt melodramatic for me to share some deep thought about a person I'd never met. Still, he was the greatest business leader of my lifetime. So I fired off a three-word tweet:

Steven Furtick @stevenfurtick   5 Oct
"What a life."

My next thoughts made my stomach hurt. Or was it the kung pao? Either way, I got downright introspective. I was wrestling with a tension:

Steve Jobs was a great man. He changed the world through technology.

I'm a pastor. I have a mission to change the world through the gospel.

But am I really achieving that mission? I'm doing well by some standards, I guess.

I love Jesus. I have integrity. I love my family.

But still…

I'm not redefining an industry. I'm not accomplishing one of the greatest feats in human history. So what am I really doing? That matters? That will matter?

That will set my life apart?

In short, I was processing the nauseating feeling that, when I stack it all up, I don't feel like I'm anything close to being the *great* man of God I want to be. Some days, actually, I feel like I sort of suck as a Christian. I didn't tweet any of that. But I couldn't stop thinking it.

I'm guessing you've had thoughts like that too. I'm not saying you want to be the next Steve Jobs or build your own technology empire. But I think we all have these honest moments when we're gripped by a desire to feel that what we're doing matters more. That who we *are* matters more.

A few hours later, after I tucked my boys into bed and prayed for them, I sat on my bed and opened my MacBook.

For some reason I felt compelled to pull up a certain Bible verse. It's one of the most staggering statements Jesus ever made.

> I tell you the truth, anyone who has faith in me will do what I have been doing. He will do even *greater* things than these, because I am going to the Father. (John 14:12)

I'd read that verse so many times. But I had a new context for it.

And it sliced me with the edge of fresh challenge.

Greater things than Jesus, the greatest man who ever lived? What does that even mean? How can we do greater *things than* Jesus?

Does it mean that we're able to do more powerful miracles than Jesus? Have a bigger impact than Jesus? I don't think so. After all, I don't know many people who have walked on water, multiplied fish and loaves to feed thousands, opened the eyes of the blind, or given salvation to the world.

If you're looking to be greater than Jesus, put down your crack pipe, my friend. That's not happening.

By leaving and then sending His Spirit to dwell inside His followers—ordinary people like you and me—Jesus released a greater power for us to do extraordinary things on an extraordinary scale. The kinds of things the early church saw and did. The kinds of things He still wants to do today through us.

Jesus isn't calling us to be greater than He is.

He's calling us to be greater *with* Him through His Spirit within us.

Meant for More

As I tried to process the brain-bending implications of that claim, I thought through some conversations I'd had recently with people who were feeling disappointed and stuck in their relationship with God and their place in life.

I'm meeting more and more believers who are unsatisfied with the kind of Christians they're becoming and the version of the Christian life they're experiencing. These aren't bad people. They aren't gangbangers and ungodly pagans. If they were, their discontent would make more sense.

The thing is, most believers aren't in imminent danger of ruining their lives. They're facing a danger that's far greater: *wasting them.*

These are some of the very people Jesus talked about in John 14:12. People who are supposed to be doing greater works than—forget about Steve Jobs—*Jesus Christ Himself.*

Yet it's not happening. For most of us, the experience of our daily lives is a far cry from the greater works Jesus talked about in John 14:12. Or even the achievements of a luminary like Steve Jobs.

We've had some big dreams about what God might want for our lives. But so many of us are stuck in the starting blocks. Or are dragging along at the back of the pack.

We know we were meant for more. Yet we end up settling for less.

We're frustrated about where we are. But we're confused about how to move forward.

I wonder if you can relate.

What a life…

Miserable Mediocrity

We all know instinctively, even if we can't articulate it exactly, that something isn't squaring up. There's a huge gap between what God said in His Word and the results we see in our lives.

It's like we've been lulled into comfortable complacency. Then we wake up one day to find ourselves stuck in miserable mediocrity. So we tuck away any dreams and notions of the great things we'd like to do for God.

After all, we're doing good. Good enough. It kind of sucks. But it's all we know.

If that's where you are today, I need to share a strong word of warning with you.

You can't keep living like this. It's not fine for you to settle for going every day to a job you'd prefer to quit, doing decent work, being a pretty good person compared to your neighbor, paying your bills on time, and sporadically reading the Bible as though it's your guide to the great things God did in other people's lives in the past.

Baseline living is not okay. Not for a believer in Jesus.

There's a price to pay for Christian complacency. If you keep living on this level, your heart is going to shrivel. It might already be shriveling. Your dreams are going to die. They may already be on life support. Will you look up one day and be overwhelmed by the stack of regrets staring back at you? The frustration that's simmering on the back burner right now might boil over one day, and you'll be bitter about the opportunities you missed. Opportunities to be used by God, to touch lives, to get outside yourself and be a part of something greater. I know it's not easy. But don't tell me it's not possible. Jesus Himself said it was.

The fact is, we are so much better than we've become, because God is so much greater than we're allowing Him to be through us.

Fairy Tale Greatness

It's one thing to believe that. It's another to live it out.

After all, John 14:12 can seem like a fairy tale. The stuff vacation Bible school heroes and Silicon Valley icons are made of. Something that normal people like us will never attain. The president probably won't release a statement calling us the greatest *anything* when we die. And only a few people will remember where they were when the news broke. Nobody will post a blog entry about our lives on a device we invented. And we aren't exactly the caliber of Christian who ends up getting a verse in Hebrews 11.

Besides, we have to pick up the kids from school, haven't

made a dinner plan, and have a big project due at work tomorrow morning.

We have real lives to live and certainly no room in our cluttered minds for pie in the sky.

Most of the time we do well just to make a dent in the mountain of laundry or leave the house in time to beat the morning traffic. It takes everything we have just to stay on top of the obstacles thrown at us like a high-stakes arcade game, let alone climb the mountain of greatness or soar like some sort of eagle. You've seen those posters, haven't you?

Part of our problem with stepping out and being great for God is that it's painfully vague. What does it mean to be *great* for God anyway? I read a book the other day that was like, give all your money away and downsize your house, and then you'll really be great for God. I saw a preacher on television later the same day who told me I would know I'd achieved a higher level of greatness when I got more money so I'd be able to buy a bigger house and a faster car. Which one is really great: modern monasticism or *Cribs*-style Christianity? I'm confused.

What would be a truly great life from God's perspective? Becoming a missionary in Zimbabwe or running a socially conscious software business? Smuggling Bibles into Burma or winning *American Idol*? Working with crack addicts or becoming an NBA star? Or would greatness be doing more than one of those things at the same time?

See, it's one thing to talk about doing great things for God.

But how do you stick a pin in that part of the map and live there? Greatness is a slippery aspiration and a wild beast to ride if you ever get on top of it.

The fact is, that kind of greatness—the unattainable, schizophrenic kind that's always in the back of your mind but always beyond your reach—is a racket.

A Way That Actually Works

That's why I have no interest in presenting you with a plan for pursuing greatness. Instead I'm going to spend the rest of this book showing you the way to a place I call *greater*.

This isn't just some gimmicky play on words. It's a game-changing shift in how we approach God.

Let me give you a simple way to look at the tension I've been describing.

Good enough = the baseline living marked by mediocrity, being stuck in spiritual survival mode, and being controlled by complacency.

Greatness = the vague, unrealistic aspirations of doing better that don't work in real life.

Good enough leaves you stuck in stagnation.
Grasping for *greatness* leads to endless frustration.
But *greater* is a third way.

Greater = the life-altering understanding that God is ready to accomplish a kind of greatness in your life that is entirely out of human reach. Beyond Steve Jobs. Beyond what you see in yourself on your best day. But exactly what God has seen in you all along.

Personally, I've decided to give up on my aspirations for greatness and legalistic expectations of Christian perfection. Not because I've given up on getting to the place God has called me to. But because I've found a better way to get there. A way that actually *works*.

It's a way that doesn't have a lot of neon signs but that leads directly to the place in God we've always wanted to experience. A secret passageway, if you will.

I found it while digging into the scriptural account of an Old Testament prophet. I found it buried in the examples of parents, students, employees, and bosses who are finding a greater passion for God than they've ever known. I finally found the door that leads to the life I've always known God is calling me to live.

And in the pages that follow, I want us to enter that passageway together, leaving our lives of *good enough* behind once and for all. Giving up on false ideas of *greatness*. Placing all our expectations, hopes, and fears squarely on the shoulders of a God whose power is greater than our minds can comprehend. And ascending to a greater realm of God's power than we ever imagined. It's a place where impossibilities cannot coexist with God's promises.

It's not out there somewhere. It's in you right now.

It's not reserved for wunderkinds like Steve Jobs and Father Abraham.

It's the birthright of ordinary believers like you and me.

It's not a state you'll achieve one day when the kids are out of the house, or the retirement account hits a certain threshold, or a particular sin isn't breathing down your neck anymore. It's a place in God you can tap into immediately, even while the dishes are piled high in the sink and you have unpaid balances on three credit cards.

Just as Jesus told Zacchaeus He would be coming to his house that day, I want you to know that greater things are coming your way, starting now. The summons is sitting in your hands. Greater works are within your grasp.

So what do you have to do to experience it?

It begins with belief.

For now, let's just clarify our focus and prepare our hearts. I want you simply to ask the Lord, in this moment, to begin to open your eyes—*by faith*—and help you perceive that He has greater things in store for your future. As you read the upcoming section, let these simple promises stack up in your heart. These truths will be like kindling for the fire God wants to ignite in the pages to come.

But it starts here, with a question: Are you ready to open your imagination to the possibility that God has a vision for your life that is *greater*?

Greater than the labels you were given when you were young.

Greater than the cynicism that may be settling in as you're getting older.

Greater than a life spent aimlessly wandering in cyberspace.

Greater than empty earthly success that brings no eternal reward.

Greater than the shame tethered to you like a stone from the sins of your past.

Greater than the abuse you suffered at the hands of people you once trusted.

Greater than the hell you've been through in the trials of your life.

Greater than the specter of missed opportunities hovering over your bed at night.

Greater than the dreams you've dreamed for yourself.

Greater than even the greatest moment you've had thus far.

> > >

You don't have to understand the implications of all this. Not yet.

You only have to be willing to believe and press into the greater things God has already prepared for you.

I'd understand if you were tempted to write me off as just another self-help hype man, wheeling and dealing promises about a better you that won't hold up in reality. You've probably heard it all before, about how if you really believe and follow this one specific plan, you'll have a better life. A great life even.

I'd be suspicious too about someone who said those kinds of things.

But I haven't said, and don't plan to say, any of those things in this book.

Instead I want to walk you straight into the gap between the greater things God has promised in His Word and the results we see in our lives.

Since writing my first book, *Sun Stand Still,* I've been overwhelmed by the miraculous reports we've received from thousands of people all over the world. In that book I dared readers to pray audacious prayers. Now I want to show you what it looks like to live an audacious *life.*

And when you live this way—the greater way—God will empower you with:

- the *confidence* to know that nothing is impossible with Him
- the *clarity* to see the next step He's calling you to take
- the *courage* to do anything He tells you to do

You'll begin to get a real sense of what greater things God wants to do in your life. Maybe God will call you to make a major life change. Or maybe He simply wants you to come at your present life with greater passion from a fresh perspective. Either way, I'm going to show you that the pathway to God's best is paved with *faith.* And I'll give you specific, tangible steps of faith to get there.

If you choose to come this way, don't expect a final destination where you can announce, "Now I'm officially greater for God!" Because the call to be greater is the call to walk with God Himself. God's greatness will not just be working *around* you—it will start working *through* you. The result will be a life of greater effectiveness. Greater impact. Greater vision. That's why the book is called *Great…er.* Emphasis, *-er.* And it's important to embrace the joy of the journey, because the destination is a mirage.

That's the thing about God's leading in our lives. It's not static. It's not automatic. But it's imminent. And it has the potential to change everything.

> > >

God's greater vision for your life isn't based on a formula. It's built on a promise: God created you for more. We'll look closely at what the Bible says "more" looks like. You'll be inspired to dream bigger than you ever have. But you'll also be challenged to start smaller, through simple steps of radical obedience.

So if you are worn-out on cul-de-sac Christianity or self-help pseudosolutions, the good news is this: today is the day God's greater plan for your life begins in full force.

The bad news is that every Batman has a Joker. And the greater life God has promised you isn't going to show up and save the day without a fight. I should know. I'm a guy who has had a front-row seat to see God do some of the greatest things you could possibly imagine. But I'm also a guy who has had to tangle with insecurities so ugly that some days they make me feel like I'm not even a Christian, let alone a pastor.

Lesser Loser Life

In seminary I studied all kinds of in-depth theological explanations about the enemies we face in the Christian life. If you boil it all down, the Bible describes a system of evil made up of three entities: the world, the flesh, and the devil. This system comprises everything that stands opposed to God's ways and God's will. And it's all designed to bring you down and keep you down. To systematically sabotage God's plan for your life and God's purposes in the world.

I'm not trying to write a comprehensive theology here. I'm just making a point that you're probably all too familiar with: breaking out of the orbit of complacency and mediocrity requires waging war against an enemy. Surprisingly, I find over and over again that my greatest enemy of the greater life God has for me is...me.

> > >

Allow me to introduce you to my shadow side. I call it my *lesser loser life*. I probably need to open up and share a bit about where I've come from if you're going to accompany me in this journey toward a place called *greater* that I've just started to describe. Full disclosure. It only seems fair.

My lesser loser life is the opposite of everything greater that God has called me to be. I like to pretend it doesn't exist, yet it's the part of me that often seems to dominate my decisions and talks me out of my tall-walking dreams. And I'm the kind of fellow who has always had big dreams.

I grew up in a small town called Moncks Corner, South Carolina. As a kid sweltering in the summer heat of the low-country sun, I remember daydreaming about a greater life. And I can tell you this—even in my wildest dreams, nothing prepared me for what any of that would really mean.

After I went into vocational ministry, my wife, Holly, and I bounced from one small town to the next, where I preached at youth lock-ins with that unique church-gym aroma somewhere between feet and Doritos. I had a steady gig leading worship at a church in rural Shelby, North Carolina. Those were good years. But sometimes, even though the life you have is good, you're haunted by a sense that on the other side of the fence that marks off the life you're living is a greater place that God is preparing for you.

Some kids want to grow up to play in the NFL. Other little boys dream of flying airplanes or fighting fires. I guess I'm a little different. Since the age of sixteen, I have been gripped by a sense that I was supposed to start a church. I didn't know much about it, other than that it was going to be a church to reach people far from God, and it was going to be in a big city. Bigger than Moncks Corner at least. Or Shelby, for that matter.

So eventually I convinced seven young families to sell their houses, quit their jobs, and move with us to Charlotte, North Carolina, to start a church together. We prayed together, fasted together, loaded U-Hauls together, named the church Elevation, invited every stranger we met in our new city to a church with a name that was even stranger, and opened our doors. Our ambition was to preach the gospel of Jesus Christ and see a city changed by His power.

Elevation has been named one the fastest-growing churches in America every year since we started six years ago. It has grown from just eight families to more than ten thousand people in regular attendance. From a ragtag bunch of bad news bears meeting in the basement of a community center, we've become an army of believers spanning six different locations, with ministry extension sites around the world. Once, we baptized more than two thousand people in the span of two weeks. There have been more than three thousand recorded salvation decisions in the last six months alone.

It's been a great ride. And it's getting greater every day.

There can't be much in life that compares to hearing someone say, "This church saved our marriage. We had the divorce papers signed, got one of your fliers in our mailbox, agreed to give this weird-sounding church a try, and tore up the divorce papers the next morning. That was three years ago."

Or, "I was strung out on drugs before I came to this church. All my friends had given up on me. But God hadn't, and I met Him at Elevation, and I've been clean ever since."

Then there's the story I heard just the other day: "My teenagers hated church. They thought God was at best a joke. But then they came to your church, and all three of them got saved on the same day."

What could be greater than that?

✟ Confessions from the Shadow Side

You'd think that someone who has seen God do so many great things would have minimal temptation to settle for anything less. You'd think I would be a permanent graduate of God's Greater University.

Then why, as I walked out on the stage a few days ago to preach to thousands of people, did I have to literally talk to myself aloud to drown out the voice inside me speaking discouragement? It was saying, *You don't belong here, boy. You don't have anything worth saying to these people. You are nothing more than a country boy from Moncks Corner, South Carolina. You're an impostor.*

And why do I often have nightmares—in the middle of the day while I'm wide awake at my desk writing a sermon—about people in my church turning against me and deciding to go to another church in town? You'd think that someone who has seen God do the great things I've seen would have more faith. You'd think I'd be more kingdom minded and wouldn't worry about people leaving my church to go to another one. After all, it's all about Jesus, right? How much smaller could I possibly think?

I'm also the kind of guy who got up at my church a few Sundays ago and preached a fearless sermon about how we should trust God to provide in every area of our lives. And how we should give to Him generously and leave the results to Him. It was one of my greatest sermons in a while, people said. But later that night, at home, Holly casually mentioned some doctor bills we'd received that we weren't expecting. It's funny, but at that moment I didn't feel nearly as full of faith as I had on the stage just hours earlier. The more I stared at the zeros on the bill from the ear doctor who had put tubes in my younger son's ears for the second time this year, the less I seemed to believe practically the stuff I had preached theoretically.

So just hours after telling people that God will supply all their needs, my chest was covered in financial-stress-induced Cheez-It crumbs. Those crumbs, and the empty Cheez-It box on the floor that had been full ten minutes earlier, reminded me that my lesser loser life is still very much alive.

I feel it in the way I sometimes want to throttle my enemies instead of praying for them.

I feel it in the way I ignore my kids and pretend to be listening to my wife because I'm behind on the deadline for my book about being greater.

Yes, I've seen God do great things through my life. But

even with all the ways I've seen Him move, I've still had my moments. I've still had my fears. I strain to believe what God has said about who I am and what He's called me to become.

Cropping Out Condemnation

Why am I telling you all this? It's not because I'm having a "Dear Diary" moment and using you for group therapy. It's because I want to set you free to believe that, just like me, you're a person through whom God can do greater things. Even though we feel like complete screwups sometimes.

I talked about how many believers are stuck in mediocrity because they settle for *good enough.* But I think, just as often, we miss out on what God wants to do through us because we listen to the voice of the Enemy telling us, *You'll never be good enough. And God could never use someone with your weaknesses, hang-ups, secret struggles, and dysfunctions.*

<u>If the devil can't suck us into the lesser loser life through complacency, he'll trap us with condemnation.</u>

We believe God can do great things. But we crop ourselves out of the picture.

Look, I know what it feels like to read a book about the great things God wants to do and to feel like it applies only to people who are better than I am. People who pray more, know more, and have it more together than I do.

But here's the paradox: in those same moments when I've questioned my calling and wondered whether I have what it takes to make a difference, I've simultaneously been a part of something greater than I even knew to dream about.

That's the beauty of the greater way. It's all about what Jesus has already done and what He desires to do through us. Period.

Nobody does greater things for God because they've got it all together. And nobody is disqualified because they don't.

Including you and me.

God doesn't do greater things exclusively through great people. He does them through anyone who is willing to trust Him in greater ways.

I know it's counterintuitive. But in spite of all the parts of us that are anything but good, God is holding the door open to a life that is greater.

That might be hard for you to believe right now. Maybe you feel like the place I'm describing is so far away that you'll never make it there before sundown. I just want you to know that I feel that way myself almost every day.

That's why I've enlisted a guide, not only to show us the way but to carry us piggyback, if that's what it takes, into the greater future God is planning for us.

Paging Our Prodigy

As much as I respect Steve Jobs, he won't be the main character in the pages that follow. We'll be drawing from the life of the prophetic prodigy named Elisha. (Not to be confused with

Eli*jah,* the Bible character who did half the miracles Elisha did but gets ten times the airplay in sermons and books. Hopefully, we can get Elisha a little street cred starting today.)

In each chapter that follows, we'll look through the lens of different experiences in Elisha's life. Through his example we'll discover what it means to be obedient to what God is saying in our specific situations, knowing that obedience to God's voice is the only definitive path to *greater.*

However, before we can follow Elisha to the heights of a greater life, we'll need to track him down in some obscure farm fields. Long before he became a hero of faith, he was stuck in the repetitive movement of mundane living. Not performing miracles but waiting for destiny to make a cameo appearance in a predictable scene.

Elisha started out just like many of us, living under the tyranny of the ordinary, plowing hard dirt. He never launched an iPad or rolled out a Think Different ad campaign. But he did reach for something greater, and God granted it to him in a way that changed his generation. And in a way that has the potential to change us today.

Dragging Behind

There's nothing glamorous about Elisha's first appearance in the pages of Scripture. He's no miracle worker, no prophet, no sage. We see no evidence that he's even a holy or devout person.

He's just a guy plowing a field.

> He was plowing with twelve yoke of oxen, and he himself was driving the twelfth pair. (1 Kings 19:19)

Plowing is backbreaking work. Not only can Elisha taste his own sweat; he can taste the very smell of the oxen. He has dust and dung caked in his hair and coating his nostrils and lungs. When you spend every day plowing, the smells and scenery are always the same. Monday you have a ringside seat for oxen rears. Tuesday if you look out the window to your right, more oxen rears. Wednesday's in-flight entertainment? Oxen rears. Thursday you click on www.oxenrears.com. Friday's special? More crust and filth for you from master chef Oxen Rear. The next Monday you get up and start the cycle all over again. It might sound bad, but plowing with oxen pays the bills.

On the day Elisha receives the calling that ignites God's greater vision for his life, he's shuffling to the slow pace of the ordinary as he always has:

Wake up.

Get dressed.

Get the plow.

Drive the oxen.

Cough up dust.

Eat lunch.

Drive the oxen.

Cough up dust.

Get clean.

Eat dinner.

Go to bed.

Wake up the next morning.

Start all over again.

There is nothing wrong with good, hard work. Some scholars think the twelve teams of oxen belonged to a wealthy landowner and Elisha was the man in charge of them all. So what his job lacked in sex appeal, it made up for in stability. It was consistent work, consistent scenery, consistent smells, and there were days when Elisha was swept up in the intoxicating tyranny of the familiar.

But every morning as he steps into the slow crawl behind the plow, he is not just chasing the oxen's tails—he is chasing his own.

Digging Up Dull

Can you relate to that kind of work? To that kind of life?

I can. When I was a teenager, I spent my summers cutting the grass and digging the graves at the local pet cemetery. Although I never buried an ox, my routine didn't vary much:

Wake up.

Get dressed.

Grab the shovels.

Dig the holes.

Transport the beloved pets.

Bury the beloved pets.

Eat lunch.

Weed-eat around headstones.

Replace the flowers inadvertently destroyed.

Get clean.

Eat dinner.

Watch television.

Go to bed.

Wake up the next morning.

Start it all over again.

For a few summers I kept in step with the monotonous march of the ordinary. And on one level, there was nothing wrong with any of it. Every teenager needs a job.

Doing the same stuff over and over again is a good thing in many instances. Routine is a vital and biblical component of our relationship with God. It's also the key to maintaining a marriage, holding down a job, staying in shape, and achieving many other desirable goals. That's not the kind of repetition we need to be rescued from—it's a kind of discipline we should embrace.

What we need to be saved from is the kind of baseline living I talked about earlier. We've already considered some of the dangers of *good enough,* and I gave some general descriptions of what that looks like. Now let's unpack some ways to recognize it. If we can identify the trappings of *good enough,* we'll be better equipped to guard ourselves against it.

The Makeup of Monotony

Spiritual monotony works against you in several subtle ways. When it sets in, the things that used to bring energy and passion to your walk with God become duty and drudgery. When you start mindlessly plowing, activities like Bible study and church attendance begin to fall more into the "I have to" than the "I get to" category. This is where complacency incubates.

Then it spreads to other areas of your life. The way it grows is deceptive. You get stuck and comfortable in a certain lifeless routine. Then you stay there long enough to get dependent on the routine. Finally you're afraid to leave the routine even though you've grown to hate it. Or worse yet, even though God is calling you out of it.

I know a lot of really good people who would admit that, for the most part, their lives revolve around this kind of mindless plowing. See, everyone is susceptible to this diabolical trap. From the president of a Fortune 500 company who is playing it safe to make the quarterly report look good, to the college freshman who is trying to stall by changing majors for the third time in a semester, to the mom who hates the way her own voice sounds when she's fussing at her kids and nagging her husband.

For a preacher like me, it's easy to get into a rhythm of preparing sermons week after week but lose some of my personal passion for God's Word in the process. I've had weeks when, after hitting Save on my message outline for the following Sunday, it's as if the Lord said to me, *You've spent all week studying My Word to minister to others. But you didn't take a single hour to study My Word on a personal level so I could minister to you.*

Turns out preachers can lose their vision behind the oxen too.

And we can all relate to the tendency to start mindlessly plowing in our relationships. Do you ever think about the lack of true intimacy you have with the people you love the most and feel utterly disappointed in yourself? Is your marriage marked more by good intentions and tolerance than passion? Or here's one for the trendy moms—have you pinned an idea on Pinterest recently for something to do with your kids that would make for great memories, only to have your plans buried in busyness and bad attitudes? Have you come to the end of a day like that and wondered, *My God, what's wrong with me?*

Regardless of who you are and what you do, succumbing to mediocrity will sabotage your spiritual vitality. You may not notice it at first, or even for years. But sooner or later, complacent

Christian living hits the point of diminishing returns. Your life isn't tiding you over as effectively as it used to. You're frustrated and irritable. You're feeling tempted in ways you can't share with your men's group.

And you see only one solution: get back behind the plow.

But mindlessly plowing is not your future.

Your situation *is* reversible. You are not consigned to an empty existence. You can start living a greater life.

Because there's something different about today...

God Is Talking Behind Your Back

It was an ordinary day for Elisha—just like today is for you—when the predictable beat of his ordinary life was interrupted, and everything changed. The interruption didn't happen the way most of us think it should. God's interruptions rarely do. Elisha didn't go to a career fair or meet with a life coach to talk about some new possibilities. Elisha wasn't looking for a different kind of life. And get this—Elisha wasn't praying. He was doing the best he could with the life he assumed he'd been handed.

But God had been watching Elisha. Hundreds of miles away from the tyranny of the plow, God had been talking about Elisha behind his back, and the gist of the conversation was that God had something greater for him. A divine calling beyond his imagination.

Enter Elijah.

You probably know Elijah one hundred times better than

you know Elisha. He's the guy who faced down the prophets of Baal in something like a religious steel-cage match and called fire down from the heavens. Elijah is the Mick Jagger of Old Testament prophets (translation for thirteen-year-old girls: he's the Justin Bieber of Old Testament prophets).

Recently God had told Elijah to appoint Elisha as his successor (see 1 Kings 19:16). In obedience to God's instruction, Elijah makes his way to the field, searching for his successor. Elisha doesn't know it yet, but the great prophet Elijah is in his neighborhood with plans to anoint him as the nation's next prophet. After that encounter nothing will be the same. The presence of Elijah, in what seems to be an ordinary situation, will thrust Elisha's life in an extraordinary new direction.

This brings us to the crucial first step for breaking away from the inertia of *good enough*: Igniting God's vision starts with *becoming more acutely aware of God's presence in your life.* Not just generally believing that God is present in the universe but understanding how He's present in your ordinary situation, desiring to do extraordinary work in your life. In a way that's even more real, yet often less obvious, than Elijah's presence in the field with Elisha, God is present with you, watching over you, planning greater things for you.

What's your gut reaction when I say that?

For a lot of people, God's presence is abstract and theoretical. Sure, God is everywhere, but it's a different thing to believe that He's personally watching over the intricacies of your life. Maybe you're thinking there's nothing of note about your life—certainly nothing worth God's attention. The paparazzi aren't exactly waiting in the bushes to see you in your workout clothes and sell the footage to TMZ. So why should you believe that you have the undivided attention of the God who created the galaxies?

If that describes the way you feel, I want you to reflect on a few verses from one of my favorite psalms. David penned these words of assurance at a time when God seemed distant to him. The first time I read them, God's presence took on a whole new meaning to me. David wrote:

> Where can I go from your Spirit?
>> Where can I flee from your presence?
> If I go up to the heavens, you are there;
>> if I make my bed in the depths, you are there…
> even there your hand will guide me,
>> your right hand will hold me fast. (139:7–8, 10)

Fortunately, no matter how isolated you feel far out in the field, God is there. He has been with you all along. He has seen you punch the clock and stir the coffee and surf the Web and return the calls.

It shouldn't freak you out to realize that God's eyes are on you. Because He doesn't see you through eyes of disapproval or disappointment. His presence is not a sign of condemnation. It's actually an invitation. God is present with you, through His Holy Spirit, because He intends to uproot you from the tyranny of the familiar, shatter the monotonous life you've had, and take you on an adventure.

He's going places you've never been and doing things you've never done. And it all comes down to a question:

Will you follow Me into greater things?

Just as Elijah personally issued that invitation to Elisha, One greater than Elijah is issuing the invitation to you. Becoming aware of His presence is the first step to realizing His purpose.

The Cloak of Your Calling

But let's go deeper and look at *how* Elijah approached Elisha. His story shows us some powerful connections about the way God calls each of us to greater things, especially when we least expect it.

The Bible says:

Elijah went up to him and threw his cloak around him. Elisha then left his oxen and ran after Elijah. (1 Kings 19:19–20)

Did you see that? Apparently Elisha doesn't hesitate. He lets go of the plow and runs after the elder prophet.

Not that he has much time to decide. Notice that Elijah is not stopping by for coffee. He doesn't sit down with Elisha to have a leisurely chat about the weather and the kids and new plowing techniques. He doesn't ask Elisha if he's really happy doing what he's doing, doesn't ask him about his deepest, darkest secrets or what he dreamed of doing when he grew up.

And that's because he doesn't have to. God has already told him that Elisha's days of mindless plowing are about to end. Even though Elisha doesn't have a clue.

God is often working behind the scenes of your life, orchestrating His destiny for you. Even though you don't have a clue what He's up to. Just because you haven't heard God call your name or tell you specifically what to do with your life doesn't mean He's not conspiring great things for you.

I guess you could say God likes to sneak up on you.

You're marching along to the beat of the ordinary. Then one day the ordinary is interrupted by a calling. That calling can change everything, if you discern it.

Find the Beat

For me, as I sweated in the pet cemetery for $150 a week, the interruption wasn't the voice of God speaking from the grave of a golden retriever. It was the sound of Pentecostal preachers coming from my headphones. See, as a brand-new, fired-up Christian, I lugged a huge collection of recordings of my favorite sermons to work every day, and I listened to those sermons on my Walkman while I strained in the sun. Remember Walkmans? They played cassette tapes. Remember cassette tapes? They... Never mind.

The point is, I remember the sounds of old-school Bible preachers booming in my ears day after day. I would rewind those tapes to the parts I liked best. I memorized those sections word for word, breath for breath, down to the pauses and cadences the preachers had perfected. To me it sounded better than any dance beat at any club. And in the subtle intonation of my spirit, I was beginning to sense something. Something life changing: *God is calling me to be a preacher one day. I'm meant for something much more than what I'm doing right now.*

Obviously, there's nothing wrong with burying pets and keeping their resting places perpetually tidy. It built a lot of discipline into me, and for that I'm grateful. But it wasn't my greater calling.

Looking back, I can see that God used those sermon tapes to interrupt my life. To speak a future into my heart. He was stirring up in me a desire that would become my life's obsession.

Elisha's calling came through a lightning-quick encounter with Elijah. Mine came, in part, through the passion of soulful preachers backed up by Hammond B-3 organs.

How will yours come?

It depends.

I've talked to some people who sensed their calling—which may have been to start a business or pursue their vocation with greater passion—through one sentence in a casual conversation that wouldn't stop ringing in their ears. Or an experience that left an imprint in their minds that wouldn't fade away.

I've also known moms and dads who got a clear and distinct vision for the way God was calling them to raise their children, not in a brilliant breakthrough moment, but over years of slow, steady, Spirit-led impressions and observations.

I could give you hundreds of examples, because God

communicates vision differently to everyone He calls. It won't be exactly the same for you as it was for me, Elisha, or your best friend.

So how will you know when God is interrupting *your* life with this calling?

You have to pay attention to the spiritual vibrations around you.

Evaluate the "interruptions" He's using to knock you off rhythm. Examine the way God is aligning the truths in His Word with the context of your life.

Is there a message that seems to be hitting you upside the head over and over again? That's one way you can know God is trying to get through to you.

Other times you won't hear it so clearly. But if you'll position yourself in God-focused places and around God-centered people, you'll learn to hear God in greater ways over time. And that's the goal. Greater.

The ways God speaks His calling into our lives are as unique as the colors He spun when He spoke the world into existence.

The thing is, you don't have to get all wrapped up in figuring out *how* God's calling will come to you. Just be ready to respond in faith when it does.

> > >

When Elijah throws his cloak—his mantle of ministry—onto Elisha, he doesn't even talk to him. And yet more is communicated in that cloak falling on Elisha's shoulders than anything Elijah could have said over a hundred cups of coffee or a thousand hours of conversation. The cloak, a simple item fashioned out of wool or animal skin, communicates this message: "You weren't meant for this, Elisha. You weren't meant to spend the rest of your life staring aimlessly at oxen rears. God has something else for you. He wants to break you out of the tyranny of the familiar and take you into a life full of unpredictability and wonder. Your life can be greater."

The cloak spills over Elisha like a tub of ice-cold water, waking him up from the monotony of the life he had, waking him up from the tyranny of the familiar. When the prophet's cloak lands on the plowman's shoulders, it's done. Elisha has been chosen as successor to the most famous prophet in Israel's history.

But now the real choice comes. Is Elisha going to choose the greater life that God has called him to? Or spend his life looking at rears?

This is a man used to the slow rhythm of plowing with oxen, a man used to the cadence of the field. For a man whose life was built on a slow rhythm and familiar routine, Elisha does an extraordinary thing:

He takes off running.

Burn the Plows

At this point maybe in your mind you are hearing the opening notes of "I Believe I Can Fly" at your high school graduation. You're expecting me to tell you to reach for the stars. Or that you too can be the next Donald Trump (minus the thing on his head) or the next president of the United States if you just follow your dreams.

The problem is, people have read millions of books containing claims like that and never experienced any real life change. They got their hopes up, but they are still the same. You are still the same. Which leads me to ask:

If God has called all of us to do great things, then why do most people not experience them? If everyone is called to that which is *greater*, why do so many people stay stuck?

Elisha's story suggests it's because too often we pick the wrong place to begin pursuing the greater things God has for us.

In this chapter I want to show you that living the greater life doesn't start with drawing up the blueprints for the new you. Or with dreaming big dreams or imagining good things. Your greater life doesn't begin with building your dream house.

It begins with burning down your old house.

We have to start with an act of arson.

The Boldest Breakaway

When Elijah's cloak lands, dense with destiny, on Elisha's shoulders, Elisha does more than run after him. He makes sure there is nothing to run back to:

> [Elisha] took his yoke of oxen and slaughtered them.
> He burned the plowing equipment to cook the meat
> and gave it to the people, and they ate. Then he set out
> to follow Elijah. (1 Kings 19:21)

Elisha destroys—and feeds to his friends—the animals that were his only means of making a living. This seems extreme to us. After all, he could have given away the oxen with bows around their necks instead of serving them up in Crockpots. But Elisha lives in a society where ceremonial sacrifice is understood. So cooking the oxen in celebration of Elisha's newfound calling is not unprecedented. His act might have offended PETA but not necessarily his neighbors.

That leaves the bizarre part: Elisha doesn't just cook the cattle; Elisha also burns the plows. Now, when the prodigal son comes home to his father in the Luke 15 story, the father kills the fattened calf. He does not throw his toolbox onto the bonfire. But that is exactly what Elisha does—he burns the tools of his old life.

We might understand why Elisha slaughtered the oxen. But why burn the plows? Even after his neighbors had second helpings of meat loaf, somebody could have benefitted from the plows. At the very least, Elisha could have hauled the plows to the Middle Eastern Goodwill or the Israelite version of the Habitat ReStore.

Not unlike the woman's pouring out a bottle of perfume upon the head of Jesus, knowing good and well it was worth a year's wages (see Matthew 26:6–13), Elisha's act appears irresponsible, maybe even selfish.

It all seems insane—until you understand this isn't a story about how to manage farming equipment. This isn't a missed opportunity for recycling. This isn't really even about plows or oxen. Burning the plows had no practical value to Elisha or anybody else. Symbolically, though, it meant everything.

Chained to the Ordinary

Elisha is making a statement, probably as much for himself as for anybody else. He is making a decisive break from his old life, from the source of his livelihood, from everything that represents the stale stability and predictability of his life behind the plow.

He is burning Clark Kent's coat and tie so he can wear Superman's cape.

And this is where we must deviate from the usual self-help

script. It is true that God had a greater life in store for Elisha than anything he had known before. And it is true that God has a greater life in store for you than anything you have known before. But if you want to have the kind of greater life Elisha had, you have to do what Elisha did. You have to burn your plow.

Your plow is what chains you to the ordinary. It could be anything.

- A present job that's not in line with what God has called you to do
- The passionless and purposeless approach you take toward the job you have and where God is calling you to remain
- Old, small paradigms of thought about what God wants to do in and through your life
- The conscious choice to keep using your spouse's past mistakes against him or her
- A life that's a little too safe, a lifestyle that's a little too comfortable and tends to factor out God

When we consider following God in a way that would disrupt our lives, we usually try to prequalify our obedience before taking the first step. But the thing is, whether you'll see God do greater things in your life doesn't depend on having the equipment you'll need for the journey ahead. You can't get too worried about whether you've read the right books or been to the right school or have the right connections. Right now, the only equipment you need is a flamethrower (or, if that sounds too dramatic, at least a box of matches).

That's because you can't step into your new life until you first set fire to whatever is tethering you to your old life. Before you can go forward into the life God has for you, you have to offer Him every part of the life you have.

It's really a matter of surrender. Will you burn the plows? You have to be ready to say, "God, whatever the greater life You are calling me into might look like, I'm in. Whether it's a big thing or a small thing You call me to do, I believe it will be a greater thing because You're the One who is calling and You are greater than all things. Whether the greater life means leaving something behind or becoming more passionate about where I am, I've decided to follow You.

"Here's my life, Lord. It's open ended. And it's pointed in the direction of the next step You call me to take. No matter what it costs."

This is what's crazy about fully surrendering to God in this way: On the one hand, it feels as if you're losing control. Because essentially you are. But on the other hand, an amazing freedom comes from praying a prayer like that. Because when you do, your heavenly Father takes the outcome of your obedience into His responsible hands. You no longer have to carry the weight on your own.

Doing the Details

Realistically, of course, you have an awful lot invested in the life you've built. Surely you can't just start setting fire to everything. If God is calling you to *step out* and away from your job of twenty years, how will you provide for your family? If, however, He is calling you to *step up* right where you are, isn't it too late to start doing things differently?

If I had answers to those questions, I would give them to you. But I don't. And, frankly, I don't expect you to get those answers from God, at least not before you burn the plows. That's just not how He works.

Have you ever heard someone say, "I don't do details"? I hear leaders say this a lot. Something along the lines of "I am more of a big-picture person. I don't do the details." It can be frustrating to work for a person like that.

It strikes me that, in His own way, God doesn't do details. I'm not saying He doesn't care about the details—Jesus said He has numbered the hairs of your head and is aware of every sparrow that falls to the ground (see Luke 12:6–7). I can't imagine a more meticulous way of managing the universe. My point is that, while God is detail oriented, He doesn't handle details or communicate them in the way most of us would prefer. He doesn't feel obliged to walk us through every contingency or provide us with every possible warranty. He simply tells us to trust Him with the outcome, commanding us to act in faith and obedience.

God does not necessarily tell you *how* He will do it, only *that* He will do it. If you sit around waiting for Him to tell you how He is going to hold up His end before you start torching your plows, you are in for an awfully long wait. Truth be told, you are probably in for a lifetime of waiting.

And it can be frustrating to follow a God like that.

God's directions can be painfully vague and incomplete. After He tells Abraham, "Go to the land I will show you," He abruptly stops talking (Genesis 12:1). He doesn't give him a road map. He doesn't give him a detailed life plan. He doesn't give him a GPS. Only a directive: "Abraham—just go."

If you are a pragmatic person, the idea that God will often direct you in this way might make you shudder. But God wasn't being cruel to Abraham, and He's not being cruel to you. There's a good reason He doesn't feel the need to give you a navigational system. It's because He is offering to *be* your navigational system. Which one would you rather have: God's guidance as a commodity or God Himself as your guide?

He will be faithful to His end of the bargain. He'll do the *showing* if you will do the *going*. You can't think too far ahead about where you'll end up.

You can only go where He tells you to go today. When you wake up the next morning, He'll show you where to go tomorrow.

The day after that, He'll show you where to go that day.

And the day after that, and the next day, and the next day.

If He told you the whole thing at once, it would probably freak you out. Besides, He's trying to teach you how to walk by faith. And most of all, His greatest ambition in leading you into greater things isn't that you would know what to do. It's that you would know who He is. That's why the simple, uncomplicated word *go* is not the Father's plan to disorient you but His attempt to develop you. It's an imperative born out of compassion, not out of cruelty. This is God's method of teaching us to draw near to Him. And in that process, we receive so much more than just good instructions. We experience deeper intimacy with God Himself.

Walking on a Word

In the Old Testament, God told Abraham to "go."

In the New Testament, Jesus told Peter to "come" (Matthew 14:29). That's not a tough directive when you say it to your dog and all he has to do is amble over from the other side of the living room. But when you are in a boat in the middle of a terrifying storm and Jesus is standing on the water asking you to join Him, it's another matter entirely. Abraham at least got a sentence. But Peter, his insides rocking as jarringly as the boat, got only a word. Jesus didn't offer Peter a water-walking tutorial. He didn't give him any details. He didn't show him how to lean with it, rock with it, or choreograph a step-by-step plan. He offered only a command—and expected obedience. He offered Peter just *one word*.

When God is the One talking to you, one word is more than enough.

I remember hearing the German-born evangelist Reinhard Bonnke, who has spent his life proclaiming the gospel in Africa, preach this story in a provocative way. He said that when Jesus gave the instruction to come, Peter did not actually walk on the water. "Water won't hold you up," Bonnke said. "If you don't believe that, put on your swimming trunks, drive to the beach, and try it for yourself. See if that water will hold you up."

According to Bonnke, Peter didn't actually walk on the water. He went walking on the word. He stepped out onto c-o-m-e.

> > >

Do you have enough faith in your Father to act on a word? If you do, it means that even if you don't know how it's going to work out or how it's going to end, you're willing to burn whatever plow He asks you to burn and then step into the life He's designed for you.

Maybe the only word He's giving you about your marriage is *stay*. Sometimes burning the plows means eliminating your escape plan. Maybe the only word He is giving you about your future is *trust*. Maybe the only insight He has given you about your situation is *I will provide*.

If you're going to walk by faith and trust in your Father and if you're going to see your life set free from the tyranny of the ordinary, you're going to have to learn how to obey a God who doesn't do details.

But as you obey, you'll be placing the results in the hands of a God who knows every detail and who has a contingency for every circumstance you'll ever face. He did for all the Bible characters we just discussed. When you read the account of God's calling in their lives, it may seem as if God was winging it. On the surface, it might appear that His plan was to deal with the details as they came up. But God never makes up anything as He goes along. He knows the end from the beginning.

He had Abraham's destination mapped out before Abraham ever took the first step. He had His right arm outstretched to yank Peter to his feet before he ever went under.

Just because God doesn't show *you* the details doesn't mean He doesn't know them. Your Father is the micromanager of the universe. If He schedules the worm for the bird and clothes the flower in designer dress, how much more will He do for you?

Approach the greater life knowing God has worked it all out in advance. He'll give you the day's orders when you show up at the job site because He's more interested in your full obedience than your full understanding.

It's just the way He likes to work.

Souvenir Shop

Some people never get *greater* because they're not willing to leave *good* behind. There is a cost to pay. Whether it's giving up something from your past or relinquishing control of your future, you will have to make a sacrifice.

Yet simply knowing this won't change your life. You have to *do* it.

So what are the powerful symbolic connections to your present life that you need to break in order to run into the new life God is giving you?

Does it mean walking away from a secure job or a comfortable relationship?

Does it mean staying right where you are and doing what

you've been doing but giving up on the halfhearted way you've been doing it?

Does it mean making a sacrificial gift to a kingdom cause that is so big it upsets your stomach a little just thinking about it?

Does it mean giving up some familiar habits that are re-minders of the way you lived before God started dealing with you?

We are sentimental people. We like to cling to souvenirs from the places we've been and the things we've done. But when God comes to yank you away from the trappings of your lesser loser life, it is no time for sentimentality.

> > >

I learned about this when I was a teenager starting to follow Jesus for myself. At that point my CD collection was a sacred shrine in my life. A big reason for that had to do with my aspirations: I wanted to be a rock star really bad. I had a rock band—just about the only rock band in Moncks Corner. And we were pretty good. That helped me get girls, and for a non-athlete like me, this was very good. But after I made a real commitment to Christ, listening to the bands I loved became a problem. Because the messages were often contrary to the new life I was called to live, the music brought vivid reminders of what my life was like before Jesus became the center of it.

It wasn't that rock'n'roll was the devil's music and strik-ing the wrong chords on an electric guitar was on par with sacrificing a goat to Beelzebub. The music I listened to wasn't intrinsically evil. I don't think I would have burned in hell for not having the Holy Ghost program my playlist. Still, I made a decision that shocked all my friends and kind of freaked out my parents: I decided to burn all my old CDs.

When I say *burn,* I don't mean duplicate. I mean destroy. I invited my buddies to come with me into the middle of the woods, where I made a bonfire. I told the guys no, I wouldn't give them the CDs instead, and threw the CDs into the fire. I didn't hand them down or trade them in at a pawnshop, because that's not what you do when God calls you to burn the plows. I stood by willfully and watched as Jimi Hendrix and a whole host of those he influenced not only got to stand next to my fire but melt in the middle of it.

Now, I've been around long enough to know that probably a lot of Christian music out there should be burned—set on fire by the cliché police. And I know there's a lot of good in what some would call worldly music. So I'm not saying you need to go out and burn your non-Christian albums. I am saying that, for me, it was never really about the music. Those weren't just compact discs—they were plows. They were tangible, physical connections to the life I had before Jesus gave me His cloak and took me on the road with Him.

I guess my old CDs could have made decent souvenirs. But they made for an even better bonfire. Something about the smell, crackle, and sizzle of burning plows—even if it has the peculiar stench of melted plastic CD cases—is especially sweet.

And it's not a good smell just for you. Burning plows are heaven's incense, like Yankee Candles to God (now available in delightfully realistic "burnt plastic" scent).

For the families who moved from Shelby to Charlotte to begin Elevation, burning our plows meant selling our houses and moving.

For Jesus's disciples, burning the plows meant leaving their fishing nets and boats (see Matthew 4:18–22).

What is it for you?

Opportunity Cost

I'm asking you to do a lot. To take inventory of your life and actively engage with the question "What is it, God? What personal plow do you want me to burn?"

It's drastic to cut ties with the thing that is chaining you to a life you've become comfortable with. But I promise you, the real risk isn't in launching out into a new life of greater things. It's staying in your old life of the ordinary.

Maybe right now that seems like too much to ask. That's why it's important not only to count the cost of burning the plows but also to count the cost of not burning the plows.

For the rich young ruler, whom Jesus told to sell all his possessions, burning the plows was too radical, too decisive an act. That's why he walked away sorrowful (see Mark 10:22). The rich young ruler had just as much of an encounter with God as Elisha had. The only difference was that he wasn't willing to burn the plows. The real tragedy for the rich young ruler was that he would never know what he missed out on.

Right after the rich young ruler left the scene, Peter asked Jesus what he could expect to get from following Jesus. Jesus said:

> No one who has left home or brothers or sisters or
> mother or father or children or fields for me and the
> gospel will fail to receive a hundred times as much
> in this present age (homes, brothers, sisters, mothers,
> children and fields—and with them, persecutions)
> and in the age to come, eternal life. (Mark 10:29–30)

The cost of following Jesus is great. The cost of not following Him is even greater.

You'll give up a lot to pursue God's calling on your life. You'll miss out on even more if you stay in the field.

Double Portion, No Remorse

Elisha gave up a lot to chase after Elijah. But he got back something even greater.

Years after their first encounter, just before Elijah turns the ministry over to Elisha, the student asks the mentor to confer a staggering blessing on him: a double portion of his anointing.

Elijah was regarded as the most powerful prophet in the history of God's people. His miracles were unparalleled, his stories unprecedented. As he and Elisha share one last conversation, now many miles and many years from that fleeting moment when Elijah gave Elisha his cloak, they also share the rugged intimacy of a father and son. Their story together ends as strangely as it began—a chariot of fire and horses of fire separate them, and Elijah ascends in a whirlwind.

Yet as Elijah is ascending, God delivers on the very thing Elisha had asked for: a double portion of Elijah's anointing (see 2 Kings 2:9–12). It would have been remarkable enough for Elisha simply to share in Elijah's tremendous power and miracles. But God didn't want him simply to share in Elijah's miracles—God wanted to give him something greater. Greater signs, greater wonders, greater authority, greater faith.

For a guy who had spent the prime years of his life plowing with oxen, having *any* portion of what God did in Elijah would surely have been sufficient. But Elisha didn't ask for Elijah's portion. And it wasn't Elijah's portion value-sized for an additional seventy-nine cents. It was *double* the anointing.

This is quite the picture of believing God for greater.

I don't know whether Elisha had second thoughts before he committed holy arson and his anchors to the ordinary went up in flames. But I would bet anything that he didn't have an ounce of remorse later when he was doing double the number of miracles Elijah ever dreamed of.

You're not going to have any remorse either, at least not when you've taken your greater place in God and left your lesser life behind.

If you start having second thoughts and are tempted to tap out and get back to the predictable beat of the ordinary, consider what's at stake:

Greater authority and confidence in God than you've ever known

Greater clarity of your identity and your calling

Greater purpose as you approach everyday tasks

Greater joy in knowing that you're in the sweet spot of God's blessing

Greater influence over the people around you

Greater impact in the world

The sacrifice of burning plows is great. The rewards you experience on the other side of obedience are so much greater.

> > >

It's been about fifteen years since the devil-music-bonfire/ plow-burning ceremony of my youth. Just the other day I was walking onstage to preach to thousands of people at Elevation, and while our worship band was wrapping up the final song, I was leading the people in a time of singing and celebration over the top of those final notes. God's presence was powerful in the room, and as the sound of all the people shouting the name of Jesus was swirling around me, I had this thought:

I wonder if I'd be up here right now if I hadn't burned my plows half a lifetime ago?

If I'd held on to my dream of being a small-town rock star, I'd have missed out on getting to make a worldwide impact. If

I hadn't surrendered my own plans, my own hopes, and my own dreams to the Lord in exchange for His greater plan for me, I'd have missed this moment and thousands of others like it.

Thank God I burned the plows and never looked back.

One Decisive Act of Obedience

Your act of radical obedience in burning the plows will not automatically solve all your problems. It may even create some new ones. But it will lift your perspective higher to see your situation from God's vantage point. And that reality should bring you deep peace and assurance.

I can tell you this: after you've burned the plows, it's only a matter of time before you experience the double portion.

After you burn the plows, the whole world opens up to you in a different way. From a decisive act of obedience, you can discover what the greater life looks like.

Starting in the next chapter, we're going to get practical about how the greater life works and what we must do to live there.

We are going to be on the road for a while, so pack light.

You don't need to bring any souvenirs.

Digging Ditches

I've met a lot of people who knew what it was to burn plows and set out to live for God but didn't know what to do next. They prayed, they made a commitment—and they got stuck. As a pastor, I've seen it over and over again. As a man trying to live for God, I've experienced it over and over again.

I'm guessing you've made plenty of resolutions about stuff you needed to start doing or stop doing. Maybe you were going to start praying or reading your Bible more.

Or maybe you were going to stop smoking or boycott carbohydrates or stop looking at pornography or stop saying mean things about family members behind their backs. Maybe you decided to break away from a relationship you knew was unhealthy for you.

The way I see it, there are two major reasons why well-intentioned people like us get stuck after we burn our plows.

One, we don't think big enough.

Two, we don't start small enough.

> > >

I'm not trying to talk like Yoda here. Thinking big enough and starting small enough are two sides of the same coin. So I not only want to motivate you to dream bigger dreams for your life. I also want to challenge you to take realistic steps of obedience that can actually make God's vision come to pass.

Let me show you how these two ideas work in tension with each other.

I've been hammering home the point that most of us don't think big enough about who God is and what He wants to do in our lives. After all, our God "is able to do immeasurably more than all we ask or imagine" (Ephesians 3:20). It is true that we often settle for dreams and visions that are far less than those God has for us. And He wants us to experience much more. If I didn't believe that, the title of this book would be *Samer*.

So of course God wants you to believe big—it's in His very nature. I've devoted my whole ministry to inspiring people with this truth. Preacher Dwight L. Moody made a statement that I love: "If God is your partner, make your plans big." That way of thinking makes my heart race.

But we're not going to see God's bigger vision fulfilled in our lives just because we spend more time thinking transcendent thoughts. We don't attain greater things simply by lying on the couch and concentrating on the possibilities of a better life. Alas, sitting for thousands of hours with my headphones on listening to Guns N' Roses and imagining I was Axl Rose didn't translate into my being the lead singer of the world's most dangerous rock'n'roll band.

You do have to be willing to think big. But the active ingredient of God's greater work through us is our willingness to start small.

Meet my friend Lysa. Her story inspires me because it showcases how God will often launch a vision that is larger than life by bringing a person to a starting point that is small and seemingly insignificant.

Continental Confusion

Chances are, my friend Lysa is standing on a stage in a big city right now talking to thousands of women about Jesus. I guess that's why I have a hard time imagining her crawling into her closet and bursting into tears. But she insists that a few years ago she spent more than one afternoon doing exactly that. The closet was the closest thing Lysa had to a vacation from her grueling new life as a homeschool mom. Day after day she spent hours sitting at a sticky kitchen table teaching multiplication and grammar to her five children.

On one particular day she wasn't feeling any more interested in teaching the multiplication table than her kids were in learning it. She hadn't ever yearned to be a homeschool teacher. But it was the life she had been called to. And finally the stress and exhaustion overtook her. There was nothing left to do but weep.

Of course, crying in the closet wasn't exactly what Lysa

had in mind when she had stepped into the greater life God had for her. So let's back up a bit. As God's greater plans often do, it had started with a simple assignment.

Her daughter Ashley was in Brownies, and each girl in her troop had been assigned a different country to study that year. The grand finale was an end-of-the-year festival of countries. When Ashley brought home the flier for the event, featuring a concert from an a cappella Liberian boys' choir, Lysa thought it looked like a perfect candidate for a "good mom day." A few hours before the festival, Lysa pulled out the world map. "Show me where Liberia is in South America," she said to her girls. Her oldest daughter informed her that Liberia was actually on the west coast of Africa.

When they walked into the rural church where the festival was being held, Lysa—freshly informed of what continent Liberia belonged to—took a seat. As soon as the boys' choir sang their first note, Lysa was captivated. And the story behind the music was so compelling. These orphaned boys were all former "war babies" whose parents had been brutally killed in Liberia's fifteen-year civil war (many of them in front of their children). Rebel forces had gone from village to village slaughtering the men, women, and older children, leaving the infants to fend for themselves.

Yet here they were singing from the depths of their souls about the joy of the Lord. Something about their faces, radiant with unadulterated gratitude for the faithfulness of God, left Lysa undone. Would she be capable of singing that kind of praise to God if she lost everyone and everything she loved?

And that's when an impression from the Holy Spirit dropped like a bomb inside of her: "Two of these boys belong to you."

The feeling that she was supposed to adopt was so intense, yet so threatening, that she silently developed a plan to walk out the back door of the church as soon as the music ended. If she could just get back to her normal life...

But Lysa sensed that God was doing a greater thing. So she stayed.

When the event was over, she had a question for the choir director. "Hypothetically," she asked, trying to sound as tentative as possible, "if I wanted to adopt one of those boys—could that be done?"

"Just walk into that little room over there," he said. "We're having a reception. You will know how you are supposed to help."

Lysa took her three little girls in tow and walked into the reception. Soon they found themselves in conversation with two of the choirboys. And then the strangest thing happened: when they embraced her for their good-byes, the boys called her "Mom."

Later that night and for many days thereafter, Lysa took a series of small but important steps:

She talked to her husband, Art. A lot.

They prayed about what to do. A lot.

Then they attended a second concert together and *together* felt the same impression from God.

And then they knew.

God was inviting them to step into a much different life than they had ever imagined for themselves. He didn't share the details with them about what would happen along the way, much less make any promises that it would be easy.

And then they took the next small step.

They said yes.

And that is how the TerKeursts welcomed two Liberian teenagers—thirteen and fourteen years old—into their family, believing that God's greater plans were unfolding right before their eyes.

They were about to discover that with greater opportunities comes greater opposition.

How You'll Change the World Today

Academic testing showed how far behind the boys were in their education. They would both have to start at kindergarten. And since the state of North Carolina requires students who want a degree from a traditional high school to graduate by twenty-one years of age, time was short. The only feasible solution, Art and Lysa decided, was to homeschool the boys for two years to get them up to a middle school level. That way they would be on pace to graduate in time.

But that solution led to another big challenge. As founder and president of Proverbs 31 Ministries, Lysa was in demand as a speaker and author. Testimonies came in from all over the world about how God was using her to shape women's lives.

Now, instead of ministering to tens of thousands, she would be teaching multiplication tables around the family table in the kitchen.

A lot of people would have seen that as a lesser calling. But Lysa had been walking with God long enough to know that whatever He calls you to do is the greatest thing you can be doing at that moment.

So overnight she became a homeschool mom—to all five of her children. In place of writing and speaking to crowds, she now managed daily lessons and tests and went after the daunting task of educating two teens through six grades in just two years.

And of course Lysa was no longer doing what came naturally to her. She was no longer an expert in anything. In fact, day after day she felt totally inadequate to do what God had clearly asked her to do. Before long she felt as if she were drowning.

And that's how she ended up in the closet one day, crying her eyes out.

As she was kneeling there in the closet, a question rushed into her soul. *Lysa, are you a woman of faith?*

Yes, of course I'm a woman of faith, she answered.

And then God told her things she's never forgotten:

If you are a woman of faith, you need to live a life that requires faith. You've been talking about faith, but you are a mastermind at maneuvering so that you don't have to have any faith at all. Now go back out there to that sticky kitchen table. That is where you will live by greater faith. Teaching multiplication tables is how you'll change the world today.

Blue-Collar Faith

What I love about the TerKeurst family story is that it shows us both ends of the *greater* spectrum. The vision they received from God was big and audacious. The steps of faith they took to ignite it in their lives were small and ordinary. They were willing to believe that God was big enough to call them to something greater, even when that something hadn't been anywhere in their expectations, on their wish list, or even on their radar. But all that was just blah-blah-blah and rhetoric until they took the first step to make it happen.

In other words, a big dream without a small start is nothing but a daydream. God initiates the biggest changes in our lives through the smallest starts.

In Scripture, faith isn't just about believing and certainly not about mere thinking. Faith is about action. In fact, faith *is* action. Faith doesn't come full circle through lofty thoughts but through simple steps. It's why James so pointedly said, "Faith without works is dead" (2:26, NKJV).

Faith isn't a state of mind—it's a course of action.

Faith is work.

And no one demonstrates this kind of blue-collar, get-your-hands-dirty approach to believing God for greater things more than Elisha.

Mood Music

One thing that set Elisha apart was his ability to trust God for bigger things than anyone around him dared to believe. He looked at every obstacle as an opportunity to prove that God is greater than the confines of any situation.

But Elisha didn't just *believe* that. He *did* something about it. And Elisha's action-oriented approach teaches us that miracles aren't magic tricks. They are the divine results of small steps of faith-filled preparation.

I want to show you an incredible image in one of the first main-stage miracles Elisha performs after Elijah departs and leaves the ministry in his successor's hands. It demonstrates the principle that small steps and hard work precipitate a move of God. That human action prepares the way for supernatural favor.

It comes from 2 Kings 3, and it goes like this:

King Joram is ruling over Israel during the years when the kingdom is divided. When the king of Moab rebels against him, the frightened king enlists King Jehoshaphat of Judah and the king of Edom to help him. Their combined military force should be fearsome against the Moabites—but they almost immediately run out of water for their armies and animals. Now they are preparing to face a terrifying foe while facing an even more terrifying fate: dying of thirst.

Par for the course in Israel's history, the crisis drives King Joram to look for divine help. He isn't desperate for God, but he is desperate for a solution. King Jehoshaphat asks if there is a prophet who could consult God for them. A servant reminds him of Elisha, the artist formerly known as Mr. Plow.

So the three kings and their entourages go looking for Elisha. When Elisha sees their convoy pull up in the ancient equivalent of black Cadillacs, he isn't remotely impressed. King Joram's evil parents, Ahab and Jezebel, had ruthlessly persecuted his mentor and spiritual father, Elijah. And prophets do not have short memories when it comes to injustice. But Elisha is still loyal to King Jehoshaphat of Judah. So Elisha agrees to consult with God, but he does it with an attitude:

> Elisha said, "As surely as the LORD Almighty lives, whom I serve, if I did not have respect for the presence of Jehoshaphat king of Judah, I would not look at you or even notice you." (verse 14)

It's hard to be subtle when you're speaking for God.

And Elisha is just getting warmed up. What he says next seems eccentric, given the circumstances. Remember, these kings have troops in the desert who are dying of thirst, waiting on whatever drops of hope and instruction fall from the prophet's mouth next.

"But now," Elisha continues, "bring me a harpist" (verse 15).

Really? The nation is on the verge of collapse. You're our connection with heaven, and you want some mood music?

This actually wouldn't have been a bizarre request in Elisha's day. It was common for prophets to summon musicians who were trained to play background music. It was a practice used to facilitate a sensitivity to the presence of God. So this was pretty standard in the rider for a prophet of Elisha's caliber.

Consequently, Elisha gets his background music, and the word of the Lord begins to flow from his mouth. It's exactly what the kings had hoped to hear. Well, not *exactly*.

Blisters and Bandannas

Elisha confirms to the kings that water will flow from Edom by the time the sun comes up the next morning. Their armies and their animals will have plenty to drink. The drought is almost over. God is going to deliver Moab to His people just as they prayed for. Hallelujah, somebody?

But he tells the kings to take a small, ludicrous step first.

This is what the LORD says: Make this valley full of ditches. (verse 16)

Why would anybody in their right mind dig ditches to hold rain that isn't even in the forecast?

Because that's the way faith works. When you know God has promised you greater things, you don't wait for a sign to appear before you respond. The kings wanted a miracle. They would get their miracle. But first they got a work order: This is no time for the power of positive thinking. Tie a bandanna around your head and pick up a shovel.

It would have been great if all the army had to do was

sit around thinking hydration-related thoughts or had a few guided exercises to help them visualize the water. But that's not how God operates.

It's as if God says, "If you really believe I'm going to do what I told you I would do, get busy. Show Me your faith, and then I'll show you My faithfulness. Do your part. If you will do what I asked you to do, I will be faithful to My word.

"If you'll dig the ditches, I'll send the rain."

The entire nation must have pitched in and dug all night, because they got it done. The next morning the water arrived. As promised. As always. The newly installed ditches were full of water, the armies and animals were refreshed, and the joint army easily overtook the Moabites.

I think Elisha used the process of ditch digging to teach Israel this important paradox of great faith:

Only God can send the rain. But He expects you to dig the ditches.

> > >

We all want something greater until we have to start digging for it. Imagine yourself in the biblical script. Hard dirt. Pitch-black night. Nothing but a few sentences from an erratic preacher to guarantee that *X* marks the spot.

Still, God expects you to grab a shovel and start digging.

Does that mean you'll have to do everything? That a greater life is all up to you? Of course not. Rain is God's specialty. But God has assigned a part to you. And it involves a shovel. We are commanded to prepare for the move of God before He makes the first move. Hebrews 11:1 tells us that "faith is the *substance* of things hoped for." It's "the *evidence* of things not seen" (NKJV). Faith isn't just abstract belief in propositions. It's concrete.

Sitting in that choir concert, Lysa knew in her gut that God wanted her to adopt two Liberian boys. I believe you've already been sensing some things too. Things you *just know.* Maybe they seem ridiculous. Maybe they seem like too much work.

It took a sacrifice of hard work for a thirsty army to dig ditches all over the valley. It took sacrifices of faith and obedience for Lysa to give up a successful ministry in order to adopt and teach two boys from Africa. And it's going to take sacrifice for you to get ready for your greater life. But can you really call it a sacrifice? After all, God is only asking you to make room for a larger-than-life blessing He wants to send your way.

Dig It?

Do you have enough faith in God to dig a ditch even if you can't see any rain or hear any wind? That can be a lonely challenge to face, with no one to support you, endorse you, or tell you that you're doing the right thing. Yet God is with you, developing your spiritual muscles with every turn of the shovel.

I meet single people all the time who say, "I'm just waiting on God to send me the right person." You know what? You can't make God send you the right person, but you can *be* the right person. You can dig a ditch in a valley. You can say, "Lord, until You send the rain, until You send the right person my way, I will dig a ditch and do all I can do." That means developing character when no one else is around. That means becoming a person of integrity in the face of temptation. That might mean putting the Xbox controller down, ironing your best button-down, putting some product in your hair, and joining the greeter team at your church. Dig.

It really comes down to this: What small steps and practical preparations is God asking you to make for the greater life He wants you to live? What ditches is He asking you to dig?

You can't expect God to entrust you with a big dream if He can't trust you to make a small start.

You can't have the apostle Paul's walk with God overnight. Big dream.

But you can pray ten minutes a day beginning tomorrow. Small start.

You can't entirely mend a broken relationship overnight. Big dream.

But you can have a conversation and open the door, write the letter, make the call, say, "I'm sorry." Small start.

If your kid is far from God, you can't bring him back overnight. Big dream.

But you could start praying for him every day. Small start.

Notice what Elisha *doesn't* say; he doesn't tell the kings to dig one ditch. No singular ditch digging on this prophet's watch.

Instead, make this valley *full* of ditches. Plural.

Believe that God is going to send a lot of rain.

If we really believe God is an abundant God, ready and willing to bless our lives in greater ways than we could ever imagine, we ought to be digging all kinds of ditches. In our relationships. In our careers. In our ministries. In every area of our lives, there ought to be heavy-duty equipment on site. Moving dirt. Making preparation.

And we ought to dig ditches using every means available. We can dig ditches with our words. With our prayers. With our expectations. Even with our thoughts.

How many ditches are you willing to dig? How deep will you dig them? You're not digging alone. And it's not in vain. God has a downpour scheduled in your near future. The deeper you dig, the greater the rainfall has the potential to be.

How the Dream Works

After two years of homeschooling all five of her children, Lysa's two boys had moved from kindergarten to sixth grade and were allowed to go to public middle school. The day that yellow school bus appeared over the horizon, Lysa danced the MC Hammer dance around her kitchen.

When her son Jackson turned twenty-one, he graduated high school with a 2.79 GPA. At the end of his senior year, Lysa received a letter from his principal inviting them to the academic awards banquet. She thought it was strange for her family to be invited, since a 2.79 doesn't generally merit an academic award. So Lysa and her family sat through the ceremony until the end, baffled by their personal invitation. Until just before they closed the event, when the principal began to describe the Administrator's Excelsior Award. Normally, it goes to the student with the highest GPA. This year, he said, the faculty had decided to give the award to the student with the richest amount of character facing the greatest odds.

"This year's Administrator's Excelsior goes to...Jackson TerKeurst."

As I'm writing this, DreamWorks is negotiating with Lysa to make her family's story into a Broadway musical. The journey that started in obscurity at the kitchen table will end up being presented on one of the world's most prominent platforms.

Lysa spent many long days digging ditches in the valley. Some of them culminated in crying sessions in a closet. But now the rain is falling steadily on her life. And it doesn't show signs of slowing down anytime soon.

A Little Oil

Lysa TerKeurst is back at her day job—encouraging women through her national ministry. Her latest book has spent several months on the *New York Times* Best Sellers list.

Meanwhile, her husband, Art, owns and operates a Chick-fil-A in Charlotte. Because of his level of influence in the community, he's affectionately known as the "mayor of the Arboretum," the area of town where the restaurant is situated. Lysa says it was Art's strong leadership that enabled their family to say yes to God over and over again. Art is a great man. But while Lysa has been featured on *The Oprah Winfrey Show*, *Good Morning America*, and the pages of *USA Today*, Art is still flipping chicken.

In a book that is all about God's greater plan for your life, it really does beg the question, who's living the greater life? Is full-time vocational ministry the image of greater...and running a Chick-fil-A the image of lesser?

God forbid.

Flipping Chicken

First of all, if you've ever had the chicken sandwich (sans pickles and mayo for me, please) and finished it off with a cookies-and-cream shake, you know there is nothing lesser about Chick-fil-A. But I digress. Art has embraced his work as his ministry, and the work he does there is as transformational as Lysa's. He's not on a stage, but Art uses his profession as his pulpit every day. He invests in his workers and makes them better leaders and better people. He's known for his generosity and integrity. Basically, he uses the gifts he's been given by God to make an impact right where he is. He has no plans of leaving to pursue a greater life. He's already living it.

You see, the greater life doesn't require speaking to large crowds at conferences or hanging out backstage with Oprah. *Greater* isn't about being called to network television or international fame. And that's good, because most of us are never going to do that or have it.

Neither is the greater life always about making heroic sacrifices or doing things worthy of a Kirk Cameron special feature. It's not what we do *for* God. It's what we say *to* God—yes or no.

"Yes, God, I will follow You wholeheartedly into the greater thing You're calling me to. Whatever it looks like."

Or, "No, God, I don't want to burn my plows, dig my ditches, and follow You to a place where I have to live a life that actually requires some faith."

Yes or no. The choice is ours.

Yes will mean different things to different people. Some people will follow God into their greater lives by leaving suburban comfort zones and setting out for mission fields. That's great. And yet many, many more are called to stay right where they are and do exactly what they're doing. Not launch into something new, but take what they are already doing to the next level. That's great too.

Which one is greater?

Whichever one God calls you to do.

The great thing about God's greater vision is that you can fulfill it while flipping chicken. While you are in the twenty-third year of your marriage. While you are raising your children. Or while you are still in school and haven't gotten to any of these things yet. Greater things are possible for you—right in the place where God has positioned you. Even if you don't feel very comfortable or qualified to be there.

Green with Humiliation

Sometimes I get hit by a random wave of panic because I think I may be screwing up my kids somehow. Like I might accidentally send them out into the real world without first passing on all the basic skills. Especially when it comes to teaching guy things to my little boys. I don't hunt, fish, or fix—anything.

Currently my six-year-old, Elijah, needs to learn how to ride a bike. One without training wheels, like a lot of the other six-year-olds do. I had put off teaching him because, honestly, I didn't know *how* to teach him. And besides, to teach him to ride, first I'd have to get the training wheels off the shiny green bike I bought him for his birthday. The one that had been sitting in the garage for about a month with the training wheels still on it because I didn't know how to take them off and couldn't bring myself to ask anyone to do it for me.

The other day, though, I had one of those ten-second bursts of self-confidence. "Come on, boy," I said to Elijah. "Today's the day you learn to ride a bike." And I went to get my toolbox.

After I finally found it, Elijah half asked, half observed: "Wow, Daddy, you have your very own one of those?"

After about half an hour of sweating, straining, and suppressing cusswords, the training wheels came off. Now the easy part: teach Elijah to ride his bike without them. I could do this. I had a good dad. He taught me how to ride a bike. I'd tap those memories. Plus, I had done my homework.

But none of the stuff that Google told me about "How to teach a six-year-old to ride a bike" was working this day. I've built my whole ministry by motivating people. But after the fourth unsuccessful lap around the cul-de-sac, I realized that my full motivational powers couldn't keep Elijah's feet pedaling or his hands from squeezing the brakes for dear life or his mouth from screaming, "I don't think this is such a good idea, Daddy."

Resilient as I am, the 98 percent humidity still sucked the

optimism out of me and drove the point home: *you've met your match, Furtick.* And even though I dutifully pushed the bike back into its designated spot in the garage with a smile and promises of "We'll learn to ride soon, buddy," I had my doubts. Not about whether Elijah would ever learn to ride a bike. More about whether this little debacle was just the beginning of an onslaught of more important things I'd need to teach my boys that I wouldn't be able to figure out.

> > >

I secretly hoped Elijah would forget about our training program for a while. Maybe I could book a relative of Lance Armstrong to baby-sit one night soon and get this whole ugly thing behind me.

So when Elijah approached me at the kitchen table a couple of days later and asked, "Daddy, can you help me with something?" I dreaded what was coming next.

Until he started talking about his little brother's birthday sleepover. It was coming up in two weeks, and he needed help.

"Help with what, buddy?" I asked, relieved that the bike thing seemed to be off the table for now.

"Daddy, do you think I could preach a sermon for Graham at his birthday party?" It struck me as the best idea I'd ever heard. Then it got better. "Daddy," he said, "do you think *you* can show me how to preach that sermon?"

The Bible, the Spirit,
and Diet Mountain Dew

I felt a shot of affirmation in my veins and pounced on the opportunity to redeem myself. *Forget you, stupid green bike. You made me look incompetent last week, but right now I'm the man.*

Almost frantically, I rolled out the plan:

"Son, I'm not the best at putting things together. Or teaching you to do sports and stuff. But if you want to learn to preach, I can hook you up.

"Here's what you need to do: Go get my Bible. Then get me two huge pieces of drawing paper and at least four or five different colored crayons. One more thing: get two glasses—one for me, one for you—and get a bottle of Diet Mountain Dew for us to share, because, boy, those are the basic things you need to write a sermon. You need the Bible, you need the Holy Spirit, you need something to write with, and you need caffeine."

"Yes sir." Elijah was excited about the Diet Mountain Dew.

"And, Son, once you get all that stuff, meet me at the kitchen table. We're gonna write the best birthday sermon any four-year-old has ever heard."

He took off running and came back to the table less than a minute later with his arms full and his eyes bugging. I was even more excited but trying to play it cool.

I've written hundreds of sermons, for crowds as large as 130,000 people. But I've never written one more important than this one. Because this wasn't some silly project to occupy my kid's time. This was one of those moments when, simple as it may seem, I sensed God was revealing something important about how He had made my son and me. Our greater potential was being unleashed—to embrace what was right in front of us and to use exactly what God had already given us.

> > >

I started with "Elijah, what's your favorite Bible verse?"

"Well, they taught me Ephesians 2:8–9 in church," he said.

I said, "How does Ephesians 2:8–9 go?" I knew. I was just checking him.

He said, "For it is by grace you have been saved, through faith—and this not from yourselves, it is the gift of God—not by works, so that no one can boast."

"All right, we'll do it on those verses." I said, "That passage has the word *gift* in it. Do you think we can write a sermon about a gift since it's Graham's birthday?"

"Yeah, I think so," he said. "We could write about the greatest gift."

"The greatest gift?"

"Yeah, Jesus, the greatest gift," he said.

I said, "Yeah, we could." And then coached him a little more. "I like to have something creative when I write my sermons. So let's take the word *gift*. How many letters does *gift* have?"

He counted. "Four."

"How old is Graham going to be?"

He made the connection. "Four."

I said, "What if we made it a four-point sermon and each point started with one of the letters from the word *gift*? So it would be like g-i-f-t. Would that work?"

That worked for Elijah.

"What could the *g* stand for?" I asked.

He said, "Grace. 'Cause that word is right there in Ephesians 2:8: 'By grace you have been saved.'"

"What is grace?" I asked.

"That's easy," he answered. "They taught me that in church too. Grace is getting something good I don't deserve."

"That's it," I said. "That's what we'll tell Graham.

"Then the *i*. What can we use with the letter *i*?"

He was stumped.

"*I* is kind of a tricky one," I said. We messed with some stuff. *Intrigue* seemed a little advanced for a four-year-old's birthday party: *the intrigue of the gospel. Impartation…*no. Then I hit on an idea. "How about if we just make it 'I…have to decide to follow Jesus'?"

Elijah thought that was great. "Yeah, and then we could put something funny in there too, like, 'Trust me, Graham. I've already done this. Now you need to do it too.'" So we put that down. We put the joke in a different color.

Then I said, "How about *f*?"

"Faith," he said. "By grace through faith."

"Yeah, and what's faith?"

He was ready. "Faith is trusting God even when life seems hard," he said.

Holly was listening from the living room, and she felt compelled to inquire, "You're six, Elijah. What do you know about life being hard?"

But we put it down. "Trust in God when life seems hard."

Then I said, "And the *t* stands for 'today,' because salvation is a gift that's available today."

Elijah added one more touch. "On the last page let's write, 'The greatest gift of all is Jesus.'"

We hid the sermon in my closet and made plans for Elijah to stand on the toy box and preach it to the four-year-olds in just a few days.

You know what? We're still struggling to get the green bike up and running. Hasn't happened yet. But while we were stashing Elijah's sermon, I already had the feeling we were making one of my greatest memories of being a parent.

> > >

Who knows what other fatherhood challenges I will face in the future? I have likely blown my opportunity to impress Elijah with my mechanical skills. If he turns out to be an all-star quarterback, it will be in spite of me, not because of me. But I can help him communicate God's truth. Nobody can do that the same way I can.

In that particular moment I didn't despair over what I can't do or what I don't have. I stopped lamenting over the toolbox I can't use so that I could fully embrace the crayons and paper I most certainly can use. But more than crayons, I used what was right in front of me—my ability to preach—and watched as God ushered something greater into my son's life and into my experience as a father.

Now, I hope you don't come away from my example with this thought: *Wow, great story. I wish I could teach my kid how to preach.*

That would miss the point badly. I'm not a great dad. Not in the way you would typically define a great dad. But I've given up on being a great dad. And I've decided to be a greater dad. That means giving my kids all I have to give and making peace with what I'm not able to give. If I stay engaged in a wholehearted way to lead my family, God will see to it that my kids get all they need, despite my mechanical ineptitude.

I can always pay someone a few bucks to remove the freaking training wheels. That or I'll borrow a chain saw.

Exchanging False Expectations

God's greater purpose in any area of your life means giving up your false expectations of greatness to find the greater things He's called only you to do. It means giving up on what others can do that you wish you could do and what you would do if you had certain gifts that you, candidly, do not have and may never develop. When you embrace the limitations of your current life situation and decide to trust God completely and cooperate with Him fully in this season of your life, even greater things are possible.

Mothers, God is just as pleased when you teach your daughters how to cook as He is when I teach my kid how to preach.

When a single young lady makes the daily decision to be pure and content in the face of all kinds of pressure pushing her in another direction, that's something God can bless. It will lead to greater blessings in her future than she could ever imagine right now.

And if you're a dad who can't prepare a sermon but can assemble a bike in a tree stand while simultaneously helping your son shoot his first twelve-point buck, I salute you. You're the greatest dad in the world.

Unless you ask my kids.

I can't tell you where the greater life will ultimately lead you, but I can tell you where it starts. It starts where you are. You have everything you need to do all that God is calling you to do right now.

This isn't just my overly optimistic take on being yourself and looking on the bright side. It's exactly what Elisha says to a frightened, grieving widow who has decided she is down to zero.

What's in Your House?

After the success of his nationally heralded ditch-digging initiative, Elisha isn't the enigmatic newcomer anymore. Now he's the senior prophet in Israel. When one of his fellow prophets dies, the prophet's widow comes straight to Elisha and pours out her troubles. Not only has she lost her husband, but now the creditors are coming to take her sons away as slaves (see 2 Kings 4:1–7).

In this tragic situation it seems like the great prophet would miraculously meet her need or at least offer some encouraging words. Instead he asks a question that strikes me as bizarre:

> Tell me, what do you have in your house?
> (verse 2)

As far as bedside manners go, Elisha does not seem to excel. This woman came seeking his help, yet he begins by asking for an accounting of what she has in her house. Doesn't it seem callous for Elisha to turn the tables on her in her time of need?

Nonetheless she answers him:

> "Your servant has nothing there at all," she said,
> "except a little oil."

If there was ever a model of the lesser life, you would think this woman was it. But as it turns out, one jar isn't a bad place to start. The widow is about to find out that all God needs is all she has.

Elisha tells her what to do next.

Go around and ask all your neighbors for empty jars. Don't ask for just a few. Then go inside and shut the door behind you and your sons. Pour oil into all the jars, and as each is filled, put it to one side. (verses 3–4)

And that's what the widow does. She collects empty jars. She goes home and closes the door. And she starts pouring.

And she pours.

And keeps on pouring until every jar is filled to the brim. At that very moment the miraculous flow of oil ceases.

When she reports to Elisha what happened, he tells her to sell the extra oil to pay her debts and live with her sons on what is left.

God has supernaturally accomplished what the widow could not. He hasn't just met her need; He has exceeded it—and racked up style points for extravagance.

And how did the miracle start? It started with something that seemed to amount to nothing.

All God Needs Is All You Have

Your servant has nothing there at all…

Initially, all this woman could focus on was what she didn't have. Elisha, on the other hand, was interested in her exception.

…except a little oil.

And it was her exception that became the vessel for an exceptional miracle.

We often excuse ourselves from God's greater vision because we believe we don't have enough for God to work with. Maybe it's our lackluster training. Lack of resources. Awkward social skills. Insufficient experience.

Maybe it's a busted-up marriage or a job we're sure is meaningless.

Whatever the reason, something keeps us from realizing that what we have is more than enough for God. He has a history of using what little someone has in order to do great things that only He can do.

One of the Enemy's most effective strategies is to get you to focus on what you don't have, what you used to have, or what someone else has that you wish you had. He does this to keep you from looking in your house and asking, "God, what can You do through what I have?"

The secret is, you don't need much. All God needs to take your life to a higher level is all you have. A God who created something out of nothing can certainly create something greater out of little. God can do exceptional things with your exception.

Unfortunately, most of us operate out of an "if…then" mind-set.

If I had _____, then I would _____.

If I could _____, then I would _____.

For example:

If I could sing, then I'd use my gifts to serve the Lord.

If my children were in a different stage of life, then I could get it together.

If my church had a state-of-the-art facility, then we would grow.

If I had more money, then I could provide my family with a nicer house, and the kids would be well balanced, and my wife would be more content...

This mind-set imprisons us in the lesser loser life. We spend all our time dreaming about where we wish we were and what we wish we had and no time investing in where we are and using what we have. And so what we wish we had never comes because we never use what we do have.

You may have encountered this kind of thinking in the corporate world. It's called "thinking outside the box." It's a mantra for many who want to break out and be progressive. If we are tired of getting the same results, we're encouraged to think outside the box. And to the extent that "outside the box" means tackling challenges boldly and creatively, it's good advice. But out-of-the-box thinking can actually breed frustration instead of innovation. Why?

Think Inside the Box

I read an interesting take on this in a book called *The Houdini Solution*. The author, Ernie Schenck, points out that everybody has a box. And thinking outside that box doesn't make the box go away. It just makes you frustrated. When you're done thinking outside the box, you realize that all the ideas you just came up with are pointless because you're still very much inside the box with no way to implement them. What we call out-of-the-box brainstorming can really be more like wishful thinking.

Dreaming about how God could use you to touch lives if you could sing won't make you sing any better if you can't sing well to begin with.

Visualizing how much more ordered your home would be if your children were in a different stage of life won't make the living room any cleaner.

Churches don't grow to capacity in imaginary buildings you wish you had.

And banks don't loan money for new houses based on your desired future income.

The box is what it is.

Most of the time, it's not until we embrace our limitations that God can start to use us beyond our limitations.

For better or worse, you're stuck with your limitations. For now. And while it might be euphoric to think about life as if you didn't have these limitations, they're not going away automatically. So you have to work with them.

I'm not saying you shouldn't plan ahead and you shouldn't dream. Of course you should. But your box is never going to expand to accommodate the dreams *outside* of it until you learn to trust God *in* it.

It sounds strange, but if you really want to see God expand your vision, I challenge you to think *inside* the box.

Stop waiting for what you want, and start working what you have. This can turn your greatest frustration into your greatest potential innovation. If you'll do your part, God will begin to do what only He can do:

He'll make your box bigger.

How much money *do* you have? What talents *has* God given you? How *can* you grow your church or business with the assets and resources you currently have in place? Put that to work. And God will begin to work with it, making something much more out of it.

Think of your limitations as fish and loaves that Jesus is eager to bless. He can bless only what you bring. So bring it. And since He can multiply it to the highest power He desires, it really doesn't matter what you start with. As long as it's not zero.

What has God already placed in your hands? Or, as Elisha would ask, what do you have in your house?

Toy Box Pulpit

At the Furtick house, on the day of Graham's fourth birthday party, Elijah dressed up in his best shirt, pants, and vest, then climbed down the stairs and took hold of my Bible and my hand.

"Wanna pray, Son?" I asked, wanting him to feel a little weight in the moment. Around the corner five four-year-olds in their pj's were ready to receive a word. At least I hoped they were ready. Because there were pages of Crayola-marked notes spread across the coffee table and an upside-down toy crate on which my son would stand.

"Yes sir," he said.

We prayed, and I asked him if he was ready. He nodded. With that, we marched downstairs to where the partygoers—I mean congregation—sat on the couch.

Elijah preached. I filmed it on my Flip. I saw God making me a greater father right in the middle of a birthday party. And I didn't think about those training wheels one time.

Embracing Limitation

Just as the widow did, you need to take inventory of what's in your house. What do you have?

So you don't have the opportunity to stand onstage at a football stadium and preach the gospel like Billy Graham. Who works in your office and needs to know the love of Christ? Share it with them. And maybe your coworker will be the next Billy Graham. Probably not. But that act of obedience will lead to other, greater opportunities. And the act of opening your eyes and heart to a need around you will catapult you out of lesser living into greater purpose.

So you don't have the vacation time to take a one-month mission trip to Peru. Is there a local need your church has identified that you can contribute to this Saturday morning? There isn't one? Start something.

So you don't have the money to write a twenty-thousand-dollar check to a ministry you believe in. A fifty-dollar-per-month pledge might be just the thing to stretch your faith while making a big difference through meeting a small need.

So you don't have the experience necessary to get a new job in a more exciting field. You may be picking up some wax-on, wax-off skills and disciplines that will pave a path for your future in a way you aren't meant to understand now.

Your greatest limitation is God's greatest opportunity. God has shown this to be true time and time again throughout the pages of Scripture.

When calling Moses, God simply asked him, "What is that in your hand?" (Exodus 4:2). It was just a staff—a common tool used by a common worker for a common purpose. But God used it for something greater, transforming it into an extraordinary tool for the extraordinary purposes of turning the Nile into blood and parting the Red Sea.

When feeding the five thousand, Jesus didn't send the disciples to buy out Five Guys. He simply asked them, "What do you have?" Five loaves and two fish were more than enough (see Mark 6:30–44).

I remember hearing an old Southern gospel song that said, "Little is much when God is in it." We don't do a lot of Southern gospel at Elevation, but that pretty much sums it up.

> > >

Instead of exhausting yourself with the "if…then" mentality, what if you started looking at your life this way?

If God wanted you to have _____, He would have provided it for you.

If He wanted you to do _____, He would have made you able.

But He didn't. So there must be something greater He wants to do through your limitation. He must have something in mind that's beyond your capacity to think up on your own. That shouldn't surprise us. His ways are much higher than our ways.

Start saying yes to God right where you are. Instead of always praying, "God, bless me with more," dare to pray, "God, use what I have. Take what little I have and make it overflow."

Wasted Faith

It all sounds great. Er.

You're ready to leave the lesser life behind and open yourself up to the greater life God has for you. But I wouldn't be surprised if there are a few objections floating around in the back of your mind.

Like, what about when the rain doesn't come? What about when you're working what you've got but it just isn't working?

Then there's this: Is going after a greater life even biblical?

After all, didn't John the Baptist base his entire ministry on the motto "He must become greater; I must become less" (John 3:30)? Stands to reason it would be self-centered and egotistical and slightly, if not outright, sinful to pursue a greater life. Right?

The reason I suspect you are thinking some of these things is that I've thought them myself. Over the next few chapters, I'll address them head-on. Not always with tidy answers. But from a biblical perspective.

They are questions worth asking. I certainly don't want to

chase a greater life only to get there and find God isn't in it. And while you're in hot pursuit of God's best, I don't want you to get tripped up by experiences that may seem to contradict everything I've been saying. As we're about to discover, our questions and doubts can actually serve as some of God's greatest tools to strengthen our stakes and increase our faith.

Greater Faith, Worser Situation

We've established that the path to greater things is rarely the path of least resistance. It's not like I'm trying to sell you a used car here. I've been up-front about the challenges of living this way. And yet we have explored at length the rewards of a life of obedience, the blessings that are on the other side of doing what God asks of us. An avalanche of Scripture passages reveals the ways God honors obedience. The greater path really is the better way.

But the stark reality is this: The journey toward greater things is marked with setbacks and real suffering. Sometimes as your faith is getting greater, your situation is getting worser.

Sometimes you pray in great faith, act in great obedience—and the miracle still doesn't come. The ditch stays dry. You still have only one jar of oil. Sometimes you've done everything you know to do, and in the end you're left with a sense of disappointment with God, even a sense that God has failed you. And if you have never experienced a moment like that, well, quite honestly you haven't lived long enough.

The road to greater things is not neat and linear. It is

marked not only by the messiness of real life but also by tragedy. Sometimes the rain doesn't come the next morning as you thought it would. Now not only is your body thirsty; it's sore and stiff from digging all night. Sometimes the heavens are silent.

Maybe you've tried to think inside the box and work the marriage you have. But your spouse left you anyway. And it blew your box to pieces.

Maybe you've left behind your small and limited conceptions of God and prayed for great things, like your child's cancer to be healed. But the doctors couldn't get the entire tumor.

Maybe you've launched out in faith and started a new business, believing God called you to it. But then it failed, and you were back to square one—or worse.

In these times it is tempting to say something quaint like "All prayers are answered, just not in the ways we want them to be." But truthfully, there are also moments where there is no discernible answer.

It's baffling the way God sometimes shows up in dramatic fashion to orchestrate the most minute details of your life to get you where you are supposed to go…and then in your most dire moments seems almost absent. Those who persevere on the long and greater road will not only find themselves baffled by God's power but also at times dumbfounded by His restraint during times of real need.

The faith of all the saints through the ages is not enough to eliminate the reality of suffering. Because suffering is not a detour on the road to greater. It's a landmark. Discouragement is a marker, often not of being on the wrong path but of being on the right one.

Don't get me wrong. Like you, I'm no masochist looking to suffer. We are realists who recognize that even though we have witnessed great moves of God, we will also experience pain, dark nights of the soul, and the death of hopes and dreams.

Even great prophets like Elisha sometimes come up short.

> > >

Her promise from God is lying dead on the bed of the man who gave that promise to her. As she stares at the horror of a miracle gone wrong, she remembers the first time she met Elisha. The dead son on the bed—the bed she had made for Elisha years ago—was an agonizing confirmation of her greatest fear and deepest suspicion: those who ask God for greater things only end up disappointed in the end.

The Bible gives her no name. She is just known as the woman from Shunem or the Shunammite woman. (You'll find her story in 2 Kings 4.) Her life had been just fine until God got involved.

She is wealthy but generous of spirit. She loves to cook. So whenever Elisha's ministry travels brought him near her family's hometown of Shunem, she insisted on having him over for dinner. She and her husband loved to show their hospitality to the enigmatic prophet, making a home for a man who never seemed quite at home in this world. For the itinerant man of God, this was a safe place to experience the laughter and comfort of family, surely a welcome break from the high highs and low lows of all-consuming prophetic ministry.

Her heart was so tender for Elisha that one day she told her husband they should build a room onto their house just for him. They constructed a small roof chamber with walls and added a bed, table, chair, and lamp so Elisha wouldn't have to stay at the Shunem Motel 6. That room became a second home for Elisha.

One day as he lay in the bed inside the room built just for him, Elisha called for his servant, Gehazi, and asked him to bring the Shunammite woman. Longing to give her something for the incredible generosity she had shown him, Elisha was reminded that the woman did not have a son. So when she stood at the door, he prophesied over her: "About this time next year…you will hold a son in your arms" (verse 16).

Most people would have reacted with either unrestrained jubilation or somber gratitude. But not the Shunammite woman. A baby? It was too late for her. Her husband was too old. To anyone outside their intimate circle of friendship, her instant reply probably would have smacked of irreverence. She objected, "No, my lord. Don't mislead your servant, O man of God!"

In other words, "Don't joke with me about this, Elisha. It's not funny."

We've all been there. When you've lived with lesser long enough, any promise of a greater possibility smacks of the potential to turn out hollow.

But Elisha wasn't joking. In due time the Shunammite woman bore a son as had been prophesied. Her only son, the object of her absolute affection—she loved him in ways she couldn't have imagined.

Everyone has high hopes for their children. But what kind of hopes does one have for a son who was not supposed to be, who was born out of a word from God? Everything about that squirming, vulnerable little body was swaddled in promise. Surely the God who so mysteriously provided a son would be faithful to protect him.

I Didn't Ask for This

The morning, years later, when her son gets up to help his father among the reapers seems like any other morning. But that day out in the sun, he is overcome by a sharp, piercing pain. "My head! My head!" he cries (verse 19). Concerned but hardly rattled, his father sends him with a servant back to his mother to lie down. Surely he just needs a nap.

The Shunammite woman cradles and rocks her son, feeling the warmth of his little body—the promise of God snuggled in her arms.

Around lunchtime he dies.

> > >

With his last breath, the sweet taste of God's faithfulness turns to sand in the mother's mouth. She had long ago learned to endure the social disgrace that marked a childless woman in her culture. She had loved Elisha like a brother and had never asked the traveling mystic for anything, much less for a son. She had begged him not to deceive her with hope. Now, in a moment, she is filled with rage.

She carries her son's body to the bed they kept for Elisha. Then, after saddling her donkey, she rushes toward Mount Carmel, where the man of God lives.

When Elisha sees her, he knows something is wrong. She falls down before him and takes hold of both his feet. Gehazi tries to intervene, but Elisha stops him. "Leave her alone! She is in bitter distress," he says (verse 27).

At that point she explodes in precisely the way you aren't supposed to talk to a prophet.

> "Did I ask you for a son, my lord?" she said. "Didn't
> I tell you, 'Don't raise my hopes'?" (verse 28)

It isn't really a question. It is an accusation. It is a way of saying "I didn't ask for this."

Elisha doesn't waste a second. He tells Gehazi to take the prophet's staff and run ahead to Shunem. "If you meet anyone, do not greet him, and if anyone greets you, do not answer. Lay my staff on the boy's face," he says (verse 29).

The prophet and the woman follow behind.

What is she thinking as she travels homeward? Upset as she is, I don't think she cares if the staff-on-the-face plan is a glorified magic trick or anything else. It could be his staff, or it could be a tennis racket—who cares?—as long as she can hold her son, living and breathing again, in her arms.

Gehazi goes ahead and does as Elisha directed, and when Gehazi comes back to meet the woman and Elisha, I think hope has already risen again, along with the color in her face.

Anticipation rises. Faith bubbles up. Not looking her in the eye, Gehazi delivers the report with dazzling understatement: "The boy has not awakened" (verse 31).

Curse you, Elisha.

> > >

Sometimes people hear from God, or think they hear from God, and they burn their plows. Or they dig their ditches. Or they pour the one jar of oil. And instead of being given beauty for ashes, they are given ashes for ashes. All they seem to get for burning their plows is the smell of smoke in their clothes. All they seem to get for digging ditches is muscle spasms for weeks to come. And pouring out their little bit of oil doesn't fill more vessels but only wastes what precious oil they had to begin with.

When God asks for something and you don't get anything back, it can feel like sacrifice. Or it can feel like you just got robbed.

I know a guy who felt certain God had called him to full-time vocational ministry, so he quit his comfortable job in the music business. He wasn't chasing fame and fortune. His heart was as pure as it could have been. But his decision cost his family dearly and created tension between him and his wife. After years of languishing, long after burning every plow he ever had, he went back to his former business, embarrassed and unrewarded. He had to provide for his family.

One of my closest friends in ministry and his wife have been married many years without children. For years they longed for kids, but finally they came to feel at peace with the idea of never having any. Their lives have been rich and fulfilling, populated with many spiritual sons and daughters. They were content with the apparent fact that biological parenthood was not God's route for them—until people all around them began to share words of alleged prophecy from God about the child they would bear. Sincere women regularly accost my friend's wife, asking if she is okay with not having kids. Some who barely know her ask if she has physical issues that keep her from having children. As their family, or lack thereof, has become a regular topic for everyone from parishioners to visiting preachers, they say it's getting hard to be okay with it anymore. And still there is no child.

I could share hundreds of heartbreaking stories about unfulfilled desires in the lives of believers. When you're a pastor, you wade waist deep in them every day. But some stories hit closer to home than others. And whether you can relate to their specific struggle or not, I think you'll find something to relate to in the story of the Bishops.

Back-and-Forth Faith

John and Heather Bishop are two of my favorite people at Elevation Church. They are one of the original couples who burned their plows and moved to Charlotte with us to start our church. John built the first deck I had on the back of my house. I take great joy in frequently giving him a hard time about overcharging me for it, but it was a nice deck. Heather was the first ministry assistant I ever had. She also ran the children's ministry and the entire church office while managing to put up with me. She did it all gracefully. I love the Bishops.

So when they struggled with fertility issues for several years, it wasn't just a general prayer request in our church. It was a personal call to faith for Holly and me—to believe God on behalf of this couple who are so precious to us. I remember how nervous I was when my wife laid her hands on Heather at a staff retreat and asked God in bold faith to give the Bishops a baby. I asked Holly in the car on the way home, "Did you have to pray that one out loud, so specifically, in front of people?"

"I felt like God told me to," she replied. Then she smiled at me. That was the end of that conversation.

I was relieved, and Holly was vindicated, when Heather announced in 2007 that she was pregnant. The struggle was over now, wasn't it? It certainly seemed that way. The Bishops bore a son. They named him Jeremiah. He was completely healthy and very handsome. And the Bishops were elated. They weren't the only ones.

Six months later, full of expectation, they began trying to conceive again. After all, once you've seen God do greater things, it's addictive to believe Him for more. Remarkably, Heather was reading the Shunammite's initial promise of a son from 2 Kings when she felt like God supernaturally spoke to her that she would have a son in a year. And they believed. And prayed. And waited.

Nine months later, she still wasn't pregnant.

Still, the Bishops aren't the kind of people to feel sorry for themselves. They stayed busy doing God's work and enjoying the son God *had* given them. They knew they were already far more blessed than they deserved.

That same month John got on a plane with me, and we flew to Uganda to check on one of our church's international partnerships. It was John's first time in Africa. And for the entire week he was there, he was moved by the joy he saw from believers in the midst of dehumanizing poverty, by the hope he saw in communities ravaged by HIV.

On one of the last days of our stay in Kampala, while we waited at a busy intersection, John looked out the window and noticed a small boy, about eighteen months old, sitting on the sidewalk with his little hands cupped in front of him, begging for money. John rarely heard God impress anything on him more clearly than in that moment. He felt God telling him, *That boy needs a father.*

In that moment John resurrendered his plans to the Lord. He realized he had been trying to hold God hostage to his plans of having a second child their way. Now he sensed God gently trying to reveal that He had a different plan for their family.

That night, November 15, 2009, he skyped with Heather. After he told her about his experience, he came right out with it: "I think God is calling us to adopt a child."

When he got home, he and Heather had a conversation about the possibility of adoption. They were nervous—as nervous as anyone who takes a bold step of faith—but they decided they couldn't settle for less than what God wanted for them. And so they started the adoption process, deciding to adopt locally.

After months of meetings, paperwork, reference letters, and long conversations with Jeremiah about the prospect of a new baby brother or sister, they finally got the call. A mom had picked their profile, and she wanted to meet them. So on October 2, 2010, they met Karrine (not her real name). In spite of their fears, they bonded with her instantly. It just felt right. The baby's due date was November 15—the one-year anniversary of the Skype conversation John had with Heather when they solidified their desire to adopt. It all seemed so perfect, what some call a "God thing."

A few weeks later John and Heather got the call that Karrine was in labor. They went to the hospital and helped her through the entire delivery. It was overwhelming for all of them. The Bishops wept on Karrine's shoulder after the baby was born. She hugged John and said she knew she had made the right choice. She was glad he was going to be her baby's father. Together, they named him Malachi David Bishop.

A few days later John and Heather brought Malachi home from the hospital. They had waited two and a half years. Struggled through infertility. Wrestled with doubts, frustration, anxiety, anger, and resentment. And now God had blessed them with the baby they'd been praying for.

I wish I could say the story ended there, but as many have experienced, God's greater plans don't always go the way we would like.

>>>

On her way home from taking Malachi to his newborn doctor's appointment, Heather got a call from Karrine. She wanted to see them and the baby. Since John and Heather wanted to make the process as easy as possible for Karrine, they happily drove to her house.

But when they got there, things had changed. Karrine said everything she could think of to make a difficult situation easier, but the gist of her message to them was that she could not be away from Malachi anymore. She wanted to be his mom. She was reversing her decision, which she had a legal right to do within seven days of the delivery under North Carolina law.

Devastated and in shock, John and Heather loaded Malachi into his car seat and drove home with him. That night they sat down with Jeremiah and told him that Malachi was not going to be their baby anymore. John kissed Jeremiah on the cheek, and he asked some questions they did their best to answer. But after a while, they couldn't hold it in anymore. They broke down and wept as a family.

The next day, one week after they helped with his delivery, Malachi was taken away.

They spent the day cleaning up all the baby stuff they had

bought or received from friends. And in the midst of all the grief, they started asking God why.

Why had He let His promise be taken away from their house?

An entire winter came and went, and the Bishops didn't hear anything new from the adoption service. They started to wonder whether God really wanted them to adopt at all. They were tired. Was God's greater plan more trouble than it was worth?

Had their faith been wasted?

The Holy Ground of Grief

Because it's an issue that touches the deepest part of my heart, I've shared several stories throughout this book about parents and children. But you have your own broken dreams and broken hopes—and they may have nothing to do with a child. Perhaps you hoped for a man or woman you would meet, marry, and live with happily ever after. Perhaps you have offered prayers for healing in earnest faith and yet you lost the person you loved anyway.

I would never attempt to insert something as blasphemous as an answer into your sacred grief. When Jesus's dear friend Lazarus died, Jesus came to the scene where the sisters and the mourners were grieving. And in one of the most profound moments recorded in Scripture, the wisest teacher in history did not offer a word of explanation or even comfort. What He did was cry with His friends (see John 11:33–36). And where

God is silent, the power of His presence is most profound in how He grieves with us.

Because God meets us when we grieve, grief is not sinful but can in fact be holy ground. Now, of course, you are reading a book about God's greater plan for you—even though you already had your hopes up and then your hopes were kicked in the teeth. If you prayed…then hoped…then lost, what could possibly be the point in asking God to move in your life now? And what could possibly convince you that His plan could somehow be greater when your dreams have been unfulfilled? Or, worst of all, your nightmares have come true?

When we pray in faith for something and it doesn't happen, we naturally tend to believe our faith was wasted. That's the source of the real pain for me. It's one thing not to get what I want. Fine. But it's agonizing to feel like "Are you *kidding me,* God? I prayed, invested, believed all that time for what? For nothing, that's what."

We don't want to bother to believe ever again. We chalk it up as wasted faith.

If that's where you are, please trust me for a moment as I share one of the most comforting insights I've ever discovered about how God works. See, there have been plenty of times when I have prayed for God to do something specific and didn't get an answer even close to what I prayed for. I prayed earnestly for God to help me sell a house that continued to stay on the market for more than two years. And that was after I lowered the price three times and promised God to give whatever little bit of profit I made back to Him.

Okay. So that's a lightweight example. Here's a better one.

Ten years ago I prayed for God to heal my dad's liver cancer. I rejoiced when the transplant was successful. Only to feel a little like God was playing games with us a few years later when much more serious health problems picked up where the liver cancer left off, causing my dad to lose his livelihood, his ability to walk, and almost his sanity. Just a few months ago the diagnosis we feared was confirmed: my father, at age sixty, has ALS, also known as Lou Gehrig's disease. They've given him about one to three years to live.

I know what it feels like to ask God to move in someone's life, then slam the phone down on my desk when I get the text saying that person's situation actually took a turn for the worse. "But thanks for praying, Pastor." In those moments I feel as though I might as well have poured my faith on the floor.

But the story of the Shunammite woman's son, the story of John and Heather, the medical twists and turns in my dad's life, and your stories of dashed hopes have one thing in common. In not one of those instances did God misappropriate His children's faith.

Not an ounce of it was wasted.

Even when it seemed as if He was deaf to their prayers, He was collecting their faith and making a plan to use it in a greater way.

I think of this as a heavenly *trust fund*. And the way it can impact our view of what it means to trust God has revolutionary implications.

Trust Fund Baby

In case you haven't spent time thinking about trust funds lately, let me give you the basics. The information I'm about to share may seem a little boring at first, but stay with me—there's a powerful analogy here. Wikipedia says a trust is "a relationship whereby property (real or personal, tangible or intangible) is held by one party for the benefit of another."

A trust fund holds money aside for an individual until he or she reaches a certain age. When the beneficiary reaches that age, a trustee is responsible to make sure that the beneficiary receives what has been held in trust for him or her. A trust is managed according to the rules under which it was created. That goes for everything from the actual amount of money to the timing of its release and the method of distribution. And all of this is recorded in a legal document, usually known as the deed.

Here's what I've come to believe: God has a trust fund with my name on it. He's governing every deposit He originally made in my life. And although I haven't seen the terms or the details, He knows the exact time every resource needs to be released to me.

I'm a trust fund baby.

I don't have a deed to review. But I have God's Word to rely on. Peter talked about how God's Word gives us "very great and precious promises" (2 Peter 1:4). Paul said that "no matter how many promises God has made, they are 'Yes' in Christ" (2 Corinthians 1:20).

I'm learning that I don't have to put my unfulfilled dreams and unanswered prayers in the column labeled Wasted. I don't have to write them off as losses at the end of each year. I can trust in the Lord with all my heart and not lean on my own understanding, because He's my Trustee (see Proverbs 3:5).

Redefining Disappointment

When you begin to see God's will in this way, you will forever define disappointment differently. You never have to spend another minute wondering if you sought the Lord in vain. If you don't see the result you're praying for and you're praying in faith, then, according to God's will, He must be putting your prayers in a trust fund.

Biblically, it isn't a stretch at all to think about faith in these terms. We're talking about a solid scriptural principle, not just an intriguing analogy. For example, one of the major verses of the Bible speaks about faith in the context of currency: "Abram believed the LORD, and he credited it to him as righteousness" (Genesis 15:6).

Abraham (earlier known as Abram) believed God for the promise of an heir and a future nation that didn't exist. The Bible says God handled Abraham's belief according to a sort of divine credit system. He converted Abraham's invisible prayers, hopes, and faith into a visible answer. He gave him a son named Isaac. He made him the father of many nations. But not right away. Not by a long shot. Abraham spent years accruing faith in the trust fund. He couldn't see a single sign that God's promises would come to pass. Even though he sometimes doubted and took many major missteps in the process, he kept believing that his Trustee was faithful. It paid off in the end.

You have your own trust fund set up too. When you pray for something and that particular thing doesn't happen, who's to say God isn't taking your faith and the prayers you prayed about that situation and posting them to another account in your life that you're going to see at a future time?

I prayed that God would help me sell my house—and my house didn't sell until long after it had lost thousands of dollars in value. But maybe in seven years I'll get a deal on another house that I never could have imagined at the time. Maybe God will bless me in another way I didn't even know to expect, far beyond what my human mind could imagine. And what about all the other ways He's provided for me in the meantime? Who's to say that God wasn't taking the faith I exerted toward one prayer that He chose not to answer and applying my faith to answer another prayer that I didn't even know to pray yet?

And what about all the good things He's given me that I didn't pray for at all? Even if I never connect the dots between what I ask for and what God gives, why should that stop me from believing He is at work in the circumstances of my life with only my best in mind?

> In all things God works for the good of those who love
> him, who have been called according to his purpose..
> (Romans 8:28)

I've decided to put it all in the trust fund and turn the results over to the One whose plan is always greater than I can comprehend. There's really no other choice if I claim to have faith in Jesus. And there's no greater way to live.

It's easy for me to say that about a house that didn't sell. It's harder at other times.

I asked my dad the other day, after he'd been through a particularly painful, sleepless night, "Do you ever struggle with feeling like the prayers we've prayed for God to heal you were all for nothing?"

"If it hadn't been for God's work in my life, I would have taken my own life a long time ago. I don't even deserve to be alive, and I hurt all the time, but He's been with me through it all. And I have a hope in heaven."

Then, after a long pause: "Do you think that's for nothing?"

God doesn't always answer our prayers. Amen to that, Garth Brooks.

But God never wastes our faith.

He never has, and He never will. It's against His character. He's a reliable manager of anything that is entrusted to Him. Including our very lives.

How could we not trust Him? Honestly, hasn't He already given us more than we deserve?

Everything I have is a gift from Him to begin with. I didn't earn it, so why would I get in God's face, claiming to know what He should do with the blessings that don't belong to me in the first place? If He has promised, He'll deliver. The answer just might be something I didn't know I was asking for at the time.

Everyone experiences what seem to be unanswered prayers. But in God's economy, no one's faith is ever wasted.

God is working on our behalf even when our prayers don't seem to be working at all. Maybe one day we'll see that the greatest setbacks in our lives were actually the greatest setups to seeing God's glory in places we didn't even know to look.

Seven Sneezes

Gehazi's bad news that the prophet's staff has not brought the Shunammite's son back to life leaves one small hope. What will happen when Elisha himself stands next to the boy's body? They hurry on to Shunem.

When Elisha comes into the house, he sees the child lying in the very place where he has spent many peaceful nights after a hearty meal and heartier laughter. But the warm evenings seem like ghostly echoes. Now there is only the child lying on his bed, cold to the touch.

Elisha shuts the door on the mother and the servant and calls on his God (see 2 Kings 4:33). He stretches out over the child, "mouth to mouth, eyes to eyes, hands to hands" (verse 34). He feels the boy's body grow warm against his skin. Elisha walks around the room. Then he stretches himself on top of the boy again. Nothing...

Suddenly the child sneezes seven times and opens his eyes. Never before has snot been so holy.

Elisha summons Gehazi to call the Shunammite woman.

What do you suppose flashed through her mind when she got the call? What emotions gripped her as she rushed to the little room? What a roller coaster she'd experienced in that home— from an unexpected gift of new life to a devastating loss, from hopes soaring to hopes dashed, and now to hopes resurrected.

The Bible gives a simple account...and lets us fill in the details with our imaginations.

> When she came, he said, "Take your son." She came in, fell at his feet and bowed to the ground. Then she took her son and went out. (verses 36–37)

Seven Days of Waiting

The bizarre turn of events in the life of John and Heather Bishop, when the birth mother of Malachi took him back, forced them to lean into God. They were living through their own Shunammite season. Looking back, John now sees that God was using their trying circumstances to help them know Him in a greater way. John didn't have the emotional strength to see it at the time, but even in the middle of their darkest hour, God was with them.

Finally, on April 18, 2011, almost a year after their first adoption meeting and three and a half years after they started trying to have their second child, they got a call from their adoption counselor. A birth mom already in labor wanted to meet them. They packed their stuff and drove three hours to the hospital.

When they met the birth mom, she insisted she wasn't a crier. But she broke down and wept as soon as Heather gave her a hug.

Then they got to meet the baby. This time they decided not to bring the baby home with them. Too much was at stake to drag Jeremiah and themselves through that emotional turmoil again.

So for the next seven days they waited.

Their wait extended over Easter weekend. As they stood worshiping together that Easter with the church they had helped to start, they celebrated what God had done for them through Jesus and were filled with gratitude. Their God didn't just love them from a distance but had come near. He had experienced the same struggles they faced. God knew what it was like to lose a son. And just as Jesus had defeated death and was resurrected on Easter weekend, so He seemed to be resurrecting the dead promise in their life.

On April 27, John and Heather brought Micah Nicholas Bishop home to be their son. On that day the faith that had seemed wasted and the hundreds of prayers that had seemed dead on arrival found a second life.

Nothing Is Over

If you have come this far through the chapter and have as many new questions as you do answers, then you have understood 2 Kings 4:8–37 better than a lot of Bible scholars. It isn't a story of easy answers. For that matter, neither is John and Heather's. And neither is yours.

These are all stories about having greater faith in God's greater plan.

What we can say for certain is that faith is never wasted. What we can say for certain is that even when the worst thing happens and no conceivable hope is left, God still surprises. No promise from God is ever completely dead.

The son of the Shunammite woman, Jesus's good friend Lazarus, the widow's son in Luke 7 whom Jesus resurrected— all of them looked dead. Were dead. But then, in one instant, everything changed.

Life was reintroduced.

Hope was rekindled.

Vitality was restored.

Upon Further Review

Have you ever been watching a football game when someone challenged the ruling on the field? It usually happens because a call is close, and they need to review the play to make sure the referee got it right. Things are not always what they seem to be in the heat of the moment, especially when you're close to the action. So the on-field referee sends the play upstairs to an official in the booth. That official replays the video, looking it over from every angle, in slow motion.

Sometimes the official confirms the ruling on the field. Nothing changes. There *was* no touchdown. The receiver *was* out of bounds. Everything was just as it appeared. Sometimes.

But other times—and these are some of my favorite moments in football—*upon further review, everything changes.* Because of something the official upstairs sees that the referees on the field couldn't see, the official overturns the ruling. It was a touchdown after all. The receiver was in bounds. And the official reverses the original verdict. In some instances that means the difference between victory and defeat.

I've seen entire seasons turn around with these three simple words:

"Upon further review…"

Every dead area of your life is under further review when you send it upstairs, to the God who has a higher vantage point and sees your situation from angles you can't access.

But this is all just theory until you embrace practical ways to see your situation from God's greater perspective. He has given us so many tools and resources to position our hearts and minds above our circumstances. Every time we go to church, for instance, and worship God in community with other believers, we're gaining altitude on our adversity, seeing things God's way instead of our own. Remember, it was in a worship service that John and Heather experienced a deep assurance that God was near to them. They didn't get this revelation sitting alone in their house with the shades drawn, wondering anxiously whether God would come through. Instead they went where they knew they could draw near to God and focus on His faithfulness.

That's how you send your situation upstairs for further review—by drawing near to God and focusing on His faithfulness.

When you hide God's Word in your heart by memorizing Scripture or speak the promises of the Bible out loud over your situation, you're drawing near to God and focusing on His faithfulness.

Maybe you need to recruit a trusted brother or sister in Christ to join you in praying through your pain because, honestly, you can't muster the faith to pray about it anymore.

Or maybe you need to start praising God—even out loud—for the ways He *has* blessed you instead of dwelling on the ways He hasn't. This simple discipline of gratitude can be a life-altering shift.

> > >

What is the disappointing situation in your life that seems dead and has you feeling defeated?

Maybe a relationship in your life just fell apart.

Maybe you lost your job last year.

Maybe you've made some terrible mistakes that have cost you a lot of time and opportunity.

Whatever the situation is, it's not over as long as Jesus is on the scene.

Upon further review, He can restore the relationship.

Upon further review, He can supply all your needs.

Upon further review, He can forgive you and make you whole.

Most of us give up too soon on the greater life God has for us. Don't lose hope. With God, nothing in your life is ever beyond resuscitation. And even in situations that feel wasted, wrapped in sorrow, cold to the touch, He has the power to bring forth one thousand new lives.

Vantage Point

This is all much easier to write about than it is to live out. And the concept of a heavenly trust fund isn't something I can prove to you on paper. You could probably list dozens of reasons to doubt it and exceptions to disprove it if you wanted to.

I can't show you a spreadsheet documenting where all your prayers went over the last ten years and exactly how God invested them or explain why it was a good move on His part. If such a portfolio exists, I don't think we get to see it this side of heaven. I doubt we'd understand it even if we did.

But I've chosen to live my life believing that I belong to One whose vantage point is greater than mine.

You can too.

God is too faithful to waste your faith. He is too wise to make a mistake. He is too loving to disregard your heart. And He is overseeing every prayer you pray, making good on every promise He has made.

Saving Captain Awesomesauce

It's possible to be too great for your own good.

Does an image of a certain kind of person come to your mind when I say that? Like the girl in your high school who was drop-dead beautiful and knew it. Or Captain Awesomesauce at work, whose ego takes up the entire conference room. Or NBA players who televise their decision to take their talents to South Beach. Not that there's necessarily anything wrong with that. I'm just saying, it's fascinating.

Some people really *are* great. Full of talent. Vision. Character. Dedication. It's remarkable when you see them doing their thing—whether that's business, fitness, creativity, relationships, or a perfect cocktail of all the above. However, we've all witnessed people who were blessed with God-given talent but who sabotaged themselves because of their self-centered pride.

The problem, of course, is that whatever person we tend to think of in that category—from a flamboyant movie star to a prom-queen diva to LeBron James—the person we usually don't think of is our own selves. That's the thing about pride: it's always somebody else's problem. Pride usually applies to somebody who has better abs or a bigger paycheck than we do.

Pride is the hidden cancer that gnaws at your insides. And its hiddenness is exactly what makes it so lethal. According to Scripture, pride is the disposition of the heart that brings opposition from God:

> God opposes the proud
>> but gives grace to the humble. (James 4:6)

Sized Up Against Our Standard

What a sobering warning to those of us who desire to be great.

Yet I've built this entire book on the premise that God is calling us to be greater.

Maybe I'm showing signs of schizophrenia. If the point of this book is how to become greater, are we lining up on the wrong side of the ball altogether?

That depends entirely on our perspective and motivation. We never realize how great we're *not* until we're sized up against something infinitely greater.

And Jesus is the only true standard for the greater life.

That means, no matter how much greater we become,

we'll always stand in the shadow of One who is infinitely greater.

If we ever really saw ourselves in comparison to Christ, we'd be humbled. The truth is, one day we will actually see our Standard face to face. In that moment we all will be in the same position: on our knees and on our faces. None of us will be looking to see how we compare to the people around us.

When Jesus returns, even the greatest men and women of our generation will not lift their heads one inch higher off the ground than any other person. That's why they're the greatest men and women of our generation. They know that, compared to Jesus, their best day is pitiful. Their best efforts, futile. Their righteousness, filthy rags. Without grace, they'd be nothing.

Without grace, we'd all be nothing.

This is the paradox of the greater life. The greater we become in God, the less about us our lives become. We don't build true greatness by adding self-esteem. We build it by subtracting self-reliance so that after our pride has been stripped away, Christ in us is revealed.

The higher you rise in God, the lower you'll be willing to go, because you'll realize more and more that the purpose of the greater life isn't to bring attention to yourself. It's to bring glory to One who will always be greater.

I've noticed that from time to time God has to bring something into our lives to help us realize we're not as great as we think.

Enter Naaman, Captain Awesomesauce

Naaman was a rock star.

Second Kings 5:1 says that he was "a great man…and highly regarded, because through him the LORD had given victory to Aram." He was a national hero known for his courage. Naaman's claim to fame was that he had helped engineer a commanding victory for his country, Aram. And to top it off, although Naaman wasn't an Israelite, God was the One who had accomplished this victory through him. If "great" is what we're aiming for, it seems that Naaman should be our role model.

Captain Awesomesauce has got it going on.

But great people often have even greater needs. Have you noticed? It's not just the people who work for minimum wage or strain to make Cs or could stand to lose twenty pounds who struggle with the lesser life.

My friend Dean came over to the house the other day while I was in the middle of writing this chapter. I was in sweatpants and hadn't shaved in three days, which is typical of me when I'm trying to crank out lots of words. I also had half-empty bags of beef jerky and empty bottles of Diet Mountain Dew covering the coffee table. After Dean surveyed the scene for a minute, he asked how my new book was coming along and if I was doing okay.

I told him I was doing great. The book was flowing. And that's why I couldn't be bothered with shaving or preparing actual food for myself—because I was in the zone. Plus, Holly was out of town.

He looked relieved and said, "Good, good." Then he asked what the book was about.

A lot of people ask this when you're writing a book, maybe just to be polite, maybe because they really care. Since Dean's a legit friend, I gave him a little more description than I normally would. This book, I summarized, is for people who sense that God has something more for them but they don't know what it is. Or they feel stuck and don't know how to get to where God is calling them to be.

He shook his head and said, "Man, I really need that book."

Now, Dean is one of the most successful young guys I know. He has his own company. His own plane. Connections with lots of other CEOs and important people. He loves God, goes to church, makes lots of money, and gives lots of it away. He runs a business that Jesus would be proud of, takes his daughters out on dates...

Captain Awesomesauce indeed.

Why would a guy like Dean, decked out in Armani with his Ferragamo loafers propped on my coffee table at the end of a day of important meetings, need to read a book about igniting God's greater vision?

Yet he sat across from me, confessing, "I don't want to go through life wondering what could have been if I had really obeyed what God was speaking to me. I don't want my pride to hold me back from God's best for my life. And I'm wrestling right now with what He's calling me to do."

We talked for the next hour about some specific steps God is calling him to take that would require him to put aside his own ideals of success and achievement. He's making the choice to burn some plows, and he's doing it by faith, even though it may not make much sense from a natural perspective.

Dean is a great man who is looking for something even greater.

One thing we need to realize about God's greater way is that it's possible to have all the external signs of greatness and yet internally yearn for something greater.

The Dip

In spite of Naaman's renown, he had two serious problems. His first problem was leprosy. For a man of influence in his culture, this was the worst possible affliction. Leprosy was not only a horrendous, incurable skin disease that led to appalling disfigurement; it was also a social plague. Lepers were quarantined and died alone.

But Naaman hears about Elisha. And if there is a chance Elisha can cure him, it is worth a shot. So Naaman decides to give the prophet a visit.

And here's where we begin to see Naaman's other problem—the greater one. Pride is eating up Naaman's insides worse than the leprosy is gnawing at his outside.

We get a hint of this when we see how Naaman shows up

at Elisha's doorstep. He isn't traveling light—he arrives with horses, chariots, servants, gold, silver, ten sets of clothing, and gifts to compensate Elisha for his services. But he doesn't go into the prophet's house with these goods.

He "stopped at the door of Elisha's house" (2 Kings 5:9).

Why does he stop at the door? Because Captain Awesomesauce is a great man! And he knows in his heart that if Elisha hears, "Naaman, the great man, has come to pay you a visit," Elisha will send a stretch Hummer to pick him up and then heal him in high style.

But Elisha doesn't play that game.

Instead of indulging Naaman's expectations, Elisha sends a messenger with these simple instructions:

> Go, wash yourself seven times in the Jordan, and your
> flesh will be restored and you will be cleansed. (verse 10)

You'd think this would be the best news Naaman has heard in his entire life.

But when Naaman hears what he has to do to be healed, he flies into a rage. Dip himself in the Jordan? That filthy, muddy excuse for a river? If dipping in a river is the cure, Naaman could have chosen any river back home. They are much purer than the waters of Israel and obviously more appropriate for a man of his stature.

Apparently Naaman is the Meat Loaf of the Old Testament—he will do anything for healing, but he won't do that.

If you've walked with God any length of time, you know

that sometimes He asks us to do the one thing we absolutely don't want to do. We say:

"I will extend Your love to anybody—except that person."

"I am willing to forgive anything—except that offense."

"I am willing to go anywhere—except that place."

Why does God so often ask us to do the one thing we think is beneath us? It's not God's punishment; it's God's love. Because the key to walking in freedom is often connected to obedience in the areas of our lives where we're locked into patterns of resisting God's Spirit.

Not until God asks us to do a humbling thing do we even recognize our pride. Naaman may not have known how much he believed his own PR—"the LeBron James of Aram"—until he heard Elisha's instructions.

And now this "great" man is about to miss out on a miracle.

Naaman has become too great for his own good. If we didn't know it already, we see it clearly in a question posed by one of his servants as he is stomping away:

> If the prophet had told you to do some great thing,
> would you not have done it? How much more, then,
> when he tells you, "Wash and be cleansed"! (verse 13)

There's our almost-impossible-to-miss word again. "If he told you to do a *great* thing..." Bathing in the polluted waters of the Jordan didn't fit into Naaman's definition of greatness.

If we're only into doing the things we perceive as adding

to our greatness, it's a sure sign we haven't found the greater way.

Dreams of Dancing Candy

There comes a time in the life of every follower of Jesus when God asks us to do something that will deliver a deathblow to our pride. I know, we've already burned our plows—that's old news. I'm talking about something different from the decisive step away from our old lives. This is about the moments when God reveals that even the *good* is worthless apart from Him. The acts that cause us to see that without Him we can do nothing. And none of this is intended to embarrass or shame us but rather to make us deeply and desperately dependent on God as our one and only source.

When we started Elevation Church, God called me to go on a forty-day fast as a way to humble myself in preparation for the work He wanted to do through our church. At the time it was the most difficult thing I had ever attempted. Maybe it seems strange to you that I would tell a story about fasting in a chapter on pride, like this is the ultimate backhanded "humble brag." Like I'm trying to slip in an example about how holy I am.

But that's a common misunderstanding about fasting—that it is an activity for especially holy people. The truth is, God gives us practices like fasting for the same reason He gave Naaman a gift certificate for the spa called the Jordan River—because we all have pride like Naaman, and we all need to take decisive steps of obedience in order for God to humble us. That's why David said in Psalms, "I…humbled myself with fasting" (35:13).

Maybe you fast forty days at a time four times a year. Maybe food isn't a big deal to you. But for me, forty days without eating was a depressing deal to consider. I've heard people who secretly struggle with lying go on and on about how a forty-day fast is "really not that hard." Whatever. I like to eat—a lot.

Some people talk about fasting in elegant terms, about its being a sweet time of communing with Jesus, and about how, after all, doesn't the Bread of Life taste better than a Big Mac anyway?

I have no such experience of fasting.

I did not spend those forty days frolicking in the fields with Jesus, thinking about how sweet He is and oh how He loves us so. The only sweetness that interested me during those forty days was the M&M's that became a part of my regular visions in the night. Really. M&M's seemed to dance in my dreams, and I think occasionally I saw them while I was awake. I was so disoriented during the fast that sometimes I would wake up in the morning unable to remember if I had actually eaten the M&M's or if it was just part of a grand delusion. I would check the trash can in the bedroom for wrappers and breathe a sigh of relief when I came up clean.

I also found that you start wanting to eat things while you're fasting that you normally wouldn't want. For example, I hate onions. But I would see onions during my fast, and I'd start fantasizing: "I would like to have a bath of onions." Or rice cakes. When you're fasting, you dream about rice cakes. You'd kill someone for a rice cake.

I'm probably establishing myself as the world's worst guide to fasting. I'm just trying to be honest about how hard it can be to want to wash in the Jordan even when you're in the middle of doing it.

But I see now why God led me to go on that forty-day fast. He wanted to deliver me from some of my own Naaman-like tendencies.

>>>

As a young man, I had already preached and led worship in a variety of settings. And even though most of the settings had been nondescript in terms of worldly prestige, those who preach and teach within the church are conferred with honor and authority.

Now I was starting my own church. And I sensed that God wanted to give me a more significant platform than anything I had experienced before—not to build my name but to build His kingdom. I realized that before God could trust me to speak into more lives, He first needed to show me how weak and dependent on Him I really was. A lengthy fast shows me the truth of who I really am: an ordinary animal who can barely control my own mood or thoughts without the food

God provides, much less accomplish anything truly great in ministry apart from Christ.

Maybe you're considering asking for your money back, even though you're halfway through this book, because "Wait a minute! Nobody told me this was a book about fasting."

It's not. It's a book about exchanging our faulty foundations of greatness for a greater foundation—the very power of God. Only you know what specific instructions God might issue you. The point is, we need to learn to recognize when God is calling us to humble ourselves so that He can become greater through us. If we can't recognize and seize those moments, then our fake greatness will keep us from it.

> > >

What is the Jordan River in your life? What is the one thing about which you would say, "I will do anything God asks me to do—as long as it is not that"?

Is it that one person you said you would never forgive?

Is it the human achievement you need to defer to pursue something God values much more?

Is it that potentially embarrassing conversation you need to have?

Is it a secret sin you need to confess?

One greater than Elisha wants to have a word with you immediately. His messenger—the Holy Spirit—can show you precisely the area where you need to take the dip. And every time you come up out of those waters, you'll be ready to be used by God in a greater way than ever before.

It's Not About Jesus

Just in case you think I'm extrapolating too much from a little story about a "great" man in the Old Testament, let me share an insight I've had into the life of the greatest man in history: Jesus. It's revolutionized my idea of a life that's greater. Think of it as the Naaman antidote. If Naaman is the ultimate example of what the greater life isn't, Jesus is the ultimate example of what it is. If Jesus is "the author and perfecter of our faith" (Hebrews 12:2), then He's the best person to take us higher into the life He created and saved us for.

The more I study the earthly ministry of Jesus Christ, the more I'm struck by an irony that marked His attitude toward His life. If Jesus had published a campaign slogan, I think it would have gone something like this:

It's not about Jesus.

I am aware that in the few seconds after you read that sentence you might have considered organizing a mob with pitchforks to come to my house. We're used to hearing people say over and over that it's all about Jesus. To say anything else is heretical.

But before you contact Terry Jones to launch protests and burn copies of this book, consider what the New Testament says about Jesus's own posture when He came into the world:

[Jesus], being in very nature God,
    did not consider equality with God something to
        be grasped,
but made himself nothing,
    taking the very nature of a servant,
    being made in human likeness. (Philippians 2:6–7)

Or consider His operating mind-set while He lived in the world:

The Son of Man did not come to be served, but to serve, and to give his life as a ransom for many. (Matthew 20:28)

Perhaps most shocking, look at the attitude Jesus expressed toward His future role when the world ends and we are in His heavenly glory:

It will be good for those servants whose master finds them watching when he comes. I tell you the truth, he will dress himself to serve, will have them recline at the table and will come and wait on them. (Luke 12:37)

When you read the New Testament, it is clear that Jesus is the ultimate giver—of life, salvation, joy, and everything else worth having.

Let me say clearly and definitively: everything is for Jesus's glory. If you study the book of Revelation, you see that everybody encircles the throne on which He sits. All glory is due Him. All honor is due Him. To miss or minimize that is to miss the point of living.

But as He walked the earth, how did Jesus demonstrate the riches of His eternal glory? By getting down low. By choosing the way that made Him appear to be nothing in the eyes of people, all the while reconciling all things to Himself with a servant's towel around His waist.

It only stands to reason: *If it wasn't about Jesus, then it definitely isn't about you.* Or me. Or anyone else.

It's not about our selfish desires. Our glory. Our comfort. Our pleasure. Our greatness. Our anything. Jesus had every right to make it all about Himself but laid it all aside in exchange for true greatness—the glory of His Father. How then can we, who don't have any such right, not do the same?

The reason that Naaman—a good, honest, and courageous man—almost missed his miracle is because he thought it was about him. Thinking it's all about us is kryptonite to the greater life. In the words of the One whom it was all about / never about: "Whoever wants to save his life will lose it, but whoever loses his life for me and for the gospel will save it" (Mark 8:35).

I know this is difficult to accept and practice. Pride is the most difficult part of the lesser life to leave behind. It's the most intrinsic to us. We have a curious habit of posturing ourselves higher than the people around us.

But consider this: later in the Philippians passage referenced on the previous page, the apostle Paul taught that because

Jesus humbled Himself, God has exalted Him and given Him the name that is above every name (see 2:9–10). Because He got low, He was lifted high.

As it was for Jesus, so it is for us. The only path to greater heights in the things of God is to get lower. The lower you get, the higher God can take you. Which is why the most advantageous position you can ever aspire to is the lowest place. John the Baptist had it right in one of the Bible's greatest verses on the greater life, a verse I've already mentioned, John 3:30: "[Jesus] must become *greater;* I must become less."

Whatever greater calling and plans God has for you, at the center of it must be a radical attitude of humility and a desire to see Jesus become greater in that calling and in those plans.

There Is No Switch

The difficulty with humility is that we do not have an interior humility switch to turn off and on; we cannot simply decide to be humble. So how can we put ourselves in that position?

Entire volumes have been written on the subject. But from everything I've studied and from what I'm learning in my experience, two principles emerge that can help us stay small while God is making us greater.

1. Immediate obedience to specific instructions.

This is one of the most overlooked ways to cultivate humility in our hearts. There's something uniquely humbling about saying to God, "I'll do whatever You ask me to do as soon as You ask me."

There's something powerful about it as well. You can see this illustrated throughout the Bible:

- God gave Noah specific instructions to build an ark. Noah obeyed, and God used him to save the family who would repopulate the world after the Flood.

- An orphan named Esther risked her life by appearing before the king in response to a specific, God-inspired prompting. Her immediate obedience saved the entire Jewish nation.

- An angel of the Lord told Joseph to take Mary as his wife. Joseph obeyed and became the adopted father of the Son of God.

And those are just three instances. Consider Moses and the tabernacle, Joshua at Jericho, Gideon's instructions to reduce his army, Ruth's unswerving devotion to her divine assignment, or any of the prophets who followed the seemingly insane instructions God gave them.

God used each of these people in greater ways—as they obeyed His simple instructions.

I've found that it's often the simplest commands and acts of obedience that have the deepest and longest-lasting results. They also become the launching pads for larger assignments of faith (see Luke 16:10). Great opportunities *later* require immediate obedience *now*.

Every time I have been obedient to a specific instruction from God—even, and perhaps especially, when it didn't make sense to me—God has done something greater in my life.

The promise of 1 Peter 5:6 is absolutely true: if you will humble yourself under God's mighty hand, He will lift you up in due time.

I can testify to this: the small deprivation I experienced during my fast was nothing compared to the way God used it in my life to display how faithful He will be if I depend on Him. I didn't know it at the time, but obeying this simple instruction was one of the primary ways God got me ready for this wild ride of leading a church that would quickly grow to thousands. He did it in a way that would leave me no choice but to recognize the truth:

It's not about me.

The starting line of humility is obedience. And that obedience will look different to each of us in each season of our lives.

Is God calling you to obey a specific instruction right now? Regarding your family? Your job? Your church? Your circle of influence? Your possessions? Your future? Your relationship with Him?

Don't ever make the mistake of thinking your life is too big for you to obey a simple instruction from God. You will never outgrow the need to immediately obey anything God tells you to do. You might as well obey God now. Delaying won't make it any easier, only more complicated.

2. Keep yourself small through your daily interactions with the people around you.

There's no greater arena where our pride or humility plays out than in our relationships. Every day we're jockeying for position with other people. Trying to get our way and assert our rights over our spouses. Our coworkers. Even the people in the car in front of us.

In those situations we have a choice. We can claim our rights and assert ourselves over each other. Or we can get low and defer and serve—like Jesus. Earlier in this chapter I said that the most advantageous position you can ever aspire to is the lowest one. That's precisely the image we get of Jesus in John 13, where we see Him washing the disciples' feet.

In that moment Jesus could have claimed His rights. He could have started singing "How Great Thou Art" to Himself. Instead John's gospel says something interesting: "Jesus knew that the Father had put all things under his power, and that he had come from God and was returning to God; *so* he got up from the meal, took off his outer clothing, and wrapped a towel around his waist" (13:3–4).

Jesus had all the authority and power in the world, and He knew it. But in spite of that, He took the lowest place in the room.

Highest Power, Lowest Place

Jesus could do this because He knew who He was. He had the affirmation of His Father—"This is my Son, whom I love" (Matthew 3:17). Because Jesus's identity was secure, there was no reason for Him to be offended. He had done everything for the disciples—from feeding them to keeping them to teaching them—and He was in the process of paying the ultimate price to save them. He didn't owe them anything; they owed Him everything. Yet because Jesus knew who He was (the Son of God), and because He knew where He had come from (from God), and because He knew where He was going (back to God), He didn't have to prove Himself to anybody. He had power—all the power in the world—but He didn't need to assert it. Only insecure people do that.

Take a minute and wrap your mind around this truth: *When you have the highest power, you can take the lowest place.* Because Jesus—who *is* the highest power—is living inside us, we too can take the lowest place.

Living this way is not a sign of weakness. In this example of Christ, we see that it's actually the greatest demonstration of strength. The only way we can walk in this kind of strength is if we are absolutely confident of our identity in Christ.

The moment we stop posturing and let go of our "rights," we are in a better position for God to use us powerfully. We are able to seek the lowest position, knowing that it is God—and God alone—who has the power to exalt.

> > >

When Naaman finally lowers himself into the Jordan, it isn't just a physical descent. He is lowering himself in obedience to God's word spoken by the lips of Elisha.

And here's a fascinating detail: when Naaman rises out of the waters of the Jordan, his skin appears "like that of a young boy" (2 Kings 5:14). The word translated as "boy" also means "servant." So it isn't just that Naaman's ravaged skin has been transformed; his heart has been transformed as well. The great man has become a servant.

You must figure out what the dip into the river looks like for you. I can tell you this—the dip was required for Naaman to fulfill his destiny. The dip was required for Naaman to be whole. And it isn't optional for us either.

When God shows you where to take the dip, do it. Don't calculate. Don't second-guess. And don't delay. Do it. Now. Immediate obedience is the gateway to the greater life that few find.

Will you be one of the few?

Where Did It Fall?

In April of 1984, Frank Culpepper was diagnosed with terminal cancer. The beloved pioneer pastor and denominational executive would live only another thirty days. Within hours of receiving the diagnosis, he asked his son Raymond to take him back to Granite Falls, North Carolina, where he had been saved and had preached his first sermon.

At that point Raymond was already a prominent church leader in his own right, as pastor of the affluent Metropolitan Church of God in Birmingham, Alabama.

Deeply revering his father, Raymond wanted to fulfill this final request—but his father was gravely ill. Raymond shares the details of his father's suffering in his book *No Church Left Behind*. Among the many physical complications, Frank's abdominal cavity kept filling with fluid, requiring his doctor to drain it. He was vomiting incessantly.

Still, every few days he would insist to Raymond, "We have to go back to my Bethel, Son, and you have to take me."

In the Old Testament, Bethel was the name of the place where Jacob first met God and built an altar to mark his life-altering encounter. Frank Culpepper was too weak to get out of his chair or to go to the rest room on his own, but he was not going to die without a trip back to that rural church.

Back to Bethel

Two weeks later Frank announced to his son, "Tomorrow we are going to North Carolina." So the next day they left Atlanta and headed for Granite Falls. The journey was a nightmare of medical complications. Every two and a half hours, Frank's stomach would fill with fluid, and he would become ill. It took them two days to get to the little church where thirty-four years earlier, after a week of binge drinking, Frank Culpepper became a follower of Jesus.

As they walked into the building, Frank, with tears in his eyes, started talking to his son. He showed him the little Sunday school classroom where God had given him his first sermon, a message on 1 Corinthians 13. He told him again about how God had saved him, about his first encounter with the power of the Holy Spirit, and about the definitive nature of his call to ministry.

Recounting his testimony, the frail man began to pray, clap his hands for joy, and raise them in worship. Raymond says he felt like an intruder on a holy moment.

A few minutes later father and son climbed the narrow

steps into the small sanctuary. "This is the place!" Frank announced triumphantly. Then, pointing to a spot on the floor, he exclaimed, "Son, that's where your old daddy got saved!"

Tears streamed down his sunken cheeks. He slowly walked to the spot and dropped to his knees. He thanked God for salvation, his wife, his mother, his children, and thirty-four years of divine faithfulness. He thanked God for his church and God's call on his life. Raymond says he had never seen his father worship the way he did on that day. He watched the Holy Spirit refresh his frail body with a new strength.

Suddenly Frank stopped praying and took hold of a bottle of anointing oil from the pulpit. Raymond was not prepared for what happened next.

"Son," Frank began, "I did not ask you to bring me here just for myself. *I came to bring you!*"

For the next few minutes, face to face and eye to eye, Frank opened up his son's heart and revealed its contents. His words burned Raymond. His father had never spoken to him like this before:

"Son, you have lost the edge," he said. "You began as a pastor with a big dream, but it has been rough. Your heart is beaten up. You're discouraged. You are busy, but not very effective. You have learned how to act like a preacher, but you're empty. You've lost your burden for lost people. Your prayer life is in trouble. No tears punctuate your preaching. You're not hungry for God like you used to be. You know how to say the right things and push the right buttons; but like Samson…you don't know the Spirit is gone. The anointing is not fresh. Your fire has gone out. You have left your first love. You must get the edge back!"

Without another word, Frank anointed his son's head with the oil from the altar and laid his hands on Raymond's head, praying, "God, forgive my son. He has grown cold. He is trying to do Your work in the flesh and has forgotten it is not by might or by power, but by Your Spirit.... Don't let him waste his precious life or Your divine calling by just going through the motions. Revive my boy in the midst of his years. Give him back his edge. Amen."

"Promise me," Frank said to his son when he was finished. "Promise me you'll repent, pray through, and get your heart right! I cannot leave this place today until you promise me."

Raymond felt exposed, embarrassed, and convicted. There he was—a husband, father, pastor, and leader being told he had lost his heart for God and His cause.

But the truth pierced him.

"Yes sir," he said. "I promise." And he did.

Two weeks later his dad died. But that day of anointing, conviction, and confession, says Raymond Culpepper, changed his life.

It Just Happened

I've written a lot to enlist you into the greater vision God has in store for you. Hopefully by this point, you're all in. You've burned your plows. You're already digging ditches, working what you have, and dripping wet from your dip in the Jordan. God's plan is opening up to you in fresh new ways, and you're taking bold steps of faith into it.

And as wonderful as all of this is and as sincere as we may be, a moment comes for those of us who follow God into the greater life when, like Raymond Culpepper, we will lose the edge. We will lose our spiritual momentum and begin to backslide into the realm of the ordinary.

We're not purposeful about or even conscious of losing momentum. It's not usually cataclysmic events that make it happen. Typically our momentum slips away in the everyday activities on the rugged plains of reality. Somewhere in the busyness of everyday life, in the flurry of activity, we lose our edge. We come to a moment when, in the midst of working hard for God and doing what seems right, we realize that something is missing.

The moment can come quite unexpectedly.

You didn't realize the tank of your passion for God was below empty.

You didn't realize your affection for your husband or wife had grown stale and perfunctory.

You didn't realize the deep ache to see your friends and family come to life in Christ had waned.

You didn't notice that the dream God placed inside you to accomplish great things for His kingdom had grown dangerously distant.

You didn't know that a hurtful comment had turned into a root of bitterness in your heart.

You didn't know you were relying too much on old victories.

You didn't notice you had lost your gratitude and had started taking the blessings of God for granted.

You didn't notice you had lost your sense of reverence for what really matters.

You didn't know there was no longer any heart behind the things you used to do for God's glory.

You didn't decide to become depressed. You didn't mean to start skipping church. You didn't decide to stop speaking words of love and encouragement to your spouse or your kids. It just happened.

I wish I could sit here and tell you that the path to a greater life is one of nonstop momentum and a never-ending ascent to glory. But I can't. Greater isn't an automatic, permanent position; it's an intentional daily decision. And sometimes in the midst of our daily lives, we turn on the autopilot and forget to make the decision. We momentarily lose what we have sacrificed so much to gain and then wonder if we'll ever get it back.

The danger comes when this wondering turns to despair, and instead of taking the steps to regain what we've lost, we're tempted to give up completely.

The good news is that it doesn't have to be this way. God already has a plan to recover anything you'll ever lose long before you actually lose it. In some ways His recovery plan is custom-tailored to your situation. In other ways it's a tried-and-tested plan that anyone can follow.

I can't promise that you're never going to lose your momentum as you chase after the greater things of God. But I can promise that it's never too late to get it back.

God's Recovery Plan

In 2 Kings 6 we find a mysterious little story about Elisha helping a man who has lost his edge—literally.

At this point in Elisha's life, he is overseeing an early seminary of sorts for young prophets. One day the junior prophets come to Elisha and tell him the place where they are living is too small. The school has outgrown its facilities.

They propose a solution. What if they all go to the Jordan to collect logs, one for each of them, and then build a new place to live? Elisha tells the kids to go ahead and build dorms to their hearts' content. But one of them asks Elisha to come along, and he agrees.

Down at the Jordan, they begin chopping trees. Suddenly, while one of the junior prophets is chopping away, his ax head falls into the water.

He cries out to Elisha, "Oh, my lord, it was borrowed!" (verse 5).

This is a powerful teaching moment. The young prophet has lost his cutting edge. He doesn't know how to get it back. And all he can do is cry out.

Do you feel his distress?

Interestingly, the young prophet didn't necessarily do anything wrong to bring the trouble upon himself. He was working hard. He was pursuing God's call on his life. He seemed to be doing exactly what he needed to do. Worst-case scenario, he just got careless.

Isn't that typical of how we lose our edge with God? Usually we're just doing our thing. Swinging away. Living life. Managing endless to-do lists. Being as nice and helpful as we can to the people we love. But at some point we look up and realize, *This isn't working anymore. I'm swinging away, but my edge is gone.*

Good thing Elisha is on the scene. In the briefest of accounts, the Bible describes how the master of momentum responds to the mishap:

> The man of God asked, "Where did it fall?" When
> he showed him the place, Elisha cut a stick and threw
> it there, and made the iron float. "Lift it out," he
> said. Then the man reached out his hand and took it.
> (verses 6–7)

Notice, no doom and gloom. No berating his pupil about his irresponsibility. Instead, Elisha asks a straightforward question: "Where did it fall?"

And when he is shown the place, Elisha cuts off a stick and throws it in the water. Next thing you know, the borrowed ax head is bobbing around on the surface of the water. Elisha tells the man to take back what he had lost. And he does.

Abruptly the story ends.

> > >

It's amazing to me that this story is even in the Bible. Think about it: This is the man of God who raised the Shunammite's son from the dead. Now he's raising an ax head out of the water? This seems below his pay grade.

But I find encouragement here. God isn't present only for my epic showdowns and life-altering crises. He's also superintending my everyday struggles. No detail or circumstance in my life falls outside His concern. He cares about little frustrations that can cause me to come unhinged. And since most of our spiritual momentum is gained or lost in the everyday affairs of life, it's good to know that God is actively involved in them.

That's why I take this simple ax head story as more than just a cute metaphor for how you'd better not lose the eye of the tiger and such. It gives you and me a basic action plan for when we sense we're losing our edge. Elisha's response to the young prophet gives us simple steps to take when we realize we're swinging hard at life but our effectiveness is slipping away.

Or maybe has already sunk out of sight.

Back Where You Left It

So what's the first step to getting your edge back?

It's realizing you can't get your edge back.

That's what the young prophet did. Rather than getting a pole to fish the ax head out or constructing a dam to dry up the river, he did the simplest and only thing he could do: he cried out. He realized it was beyond his ability to restore what he had lost. His only hope was in the power of God to supernaturally give him back the ax head and relieve him of a debt he couldn't repay.

The next time you sense yourself getting spiritually dull, don't try to regain your momentum by doubling down on your self-effort. Instead, go to God. Even if you have to do it fifty times a day. He knows your weakness, and He longs to give you strength. He doesn't want to put you through a series of lab tests to see whether you are appropriately sincere. He doesn't want you to wallow in regret. He just wants you to cry out—to call to Him. He wants to give you your cutting edge back. But He requires that you stop, get honest, and ask.

I'll make a bold claim: if you cry out to God, asking Him to restore the passion that you lost, He will answer—every single time. Why wouldn't He? Do you think God wants you to go back to being stuck in mediocrity?

It's painful to realize your ax head is lost. But there's power when you realize that the ax head isn't actually gone—it's just back where you left it. And God will defy gravity in order to put it back within your grasp.

Search and Rescue

Back in the days of real video games like *The Legend of Zelda, Super Mario Bros.,* and *Contra,* I must admit I took my gaming experience very seriously. I devoured each issue of *Nintendo Power* magazine, stayed up until 3 a.m. one time to finally beat

Soda Popinski on *Mike Tyson's Punch-Out!!*, and occasionally threw embarrassing temper tantrums.

Nothing set off my ten-year-old blind rage more than when I had advanced to the end of a certain level and, just before defeating the boss, died. That meant I had to start all over at the beginning of the level. All that effort, all those hours, wasted. My face would turn red, and the veins would pop out on my forehead. I'd try to stuff it in but would end up screaming at the stupid inanimate object that had brought me such joy and pleasure just hours before.

I threw more than one controller across my bedroom and had my Nintendo privileges revoked on several occasions for this kind of behavior.

I've felt that same frustration in my gut—at a much more profound level, obviously—in my walk with Christ at times. So often I feel as if I'm zipping along, living my life, running hard to do God's will—and then, out of nowhere, I lose my flow. I hit a spiritual low. And it feels like, *Great. All that progress I was making was for nothing. I was doing so good, being so intentional, really going after the greater things God has for me. Then I slipped right back into the same lazy patterns I was in before. I lost my intensity and settled into survival mode. I let some minor setback get me off the path. Now I have to start all over.*

You should know that I don't have thoughts like this once or twice a year. I have them multiple times every single day. I have them when my prayer time sucks in the morning and when I eat too many carbs for lunch. I have them when I waste hours at night interacting with a lesser life on Twitter instead of making a greater investment in my family.

You may have had your share of these moments too. Yet if we give in to these discouraging thoughts, it's just a matter of time until that slower, sluggish, lesser loser mentality takes over. We might continue swinging away, giving the appearance of productivity. But deep down we'll know, *My edge is gone.*

Here's the beautiful secret I'm learning about the way God works: living for God is not like playing Nintendo. I don't have to go back to the start of the level when I make a mistake, lose my focus, or drift in the wrong direction. By God's grace, I simply go back and identify where I got off track.

Was it because my communication with God had a lower place on my priority scale than the three texts I needed to reply to?

Was it because I let apathy settle in and started coasting once I achieved a certain level I was aiming for?

Was it because I started approaching situations in my life with a "What's in this for me?" attitude rather than turning my attention toward the needs of others?

How about you? Where do you tend to lose it?

Or, in the words of Elisha, "Where did it fall?"

Maybe it was a word of criticism that got you off track. You got a nasty e-mail or overheard a hurtful comment, and you started to believe the bad things you were hearing about yourself.

Maybe you started relying too much on a formulaic approach to God. It became a checklist of activities you had to accomplish every day and every week rather than a living, dynamic relationship.

Maybe you started feeling entitled to things you used to be grateful for. The perks of God's goodness in your life just became part of the package in your mind.

Maybe you slipped into a mild depression because the first thing you do after hitting the snooze button a few times every morning is listen to depressing news.

Maybe you entered into bad relationships with negative people and now they're sucking the life out of you.

Maybe you started to see the blessings in your life as curses. The kids you prayed to have are now making messes in the living room. The husband you were so thankful for on your wedding day is now your obstacle to having a good day.

Where did you lose it? Where did it fall? Are you willing to participate fully with God so you can get it back? Or are you going to stand there swinging a stick with no iron on the end of it, wondering why no trees are falling down around you?

See, God is a master of recovering that which is lost. But He expects you to cooperate with Him as the lead member of His search-and-rescue team.

If you lack momentum, it's your responsibility to evaluate the situation. Pray about what's going on. And by the grace and power of God, reach out and pick up the ax head. Get back to swinging.

It is such a simple process. But sometimes it's the simple steps that have the most profound impact.

Staying Sharp

I'll be candid with you. When Elevation had its first growth spurt and grew from just a few families to over a thousand people, it was a gloriously disorienting experience. I realized for the first time the stress and pressures that come with the blessings of being a pastor. And it scared the crap out of me.

I started realizing the devil had a bull's-eye on my soul. Many pastors develop secret lives of habitual sin. Then they wind up melting down in the spotlight for the world to see, hurting a lot of people and damaging the testimony of Jesus. By God's grace, I wasn't there yet or anywhere close. But with the stress and pace of ministry, I was afraid I could be one day. And I feared that some lingering dysfunctions inside me would eventually keep me from making the impact God desired me to have for Him. The last thing I wanted to do with my life was to set out to help people and then end up hurting thousands of people because of a lack of integrity or an unresolved issue in my life.

So about a year after we had started the church, I decided to cold-call a professional Christian counselor. Who else do you talk to when you're the pastor? You don't have a pastor to bring your burdens to because, well, you're it.

That phone call was pretty awkward. I spoke in hushed tones in my office because I didn't want any other staff members to overhear. When this guy Lance picked up the phone, I told him I wanted to meet with him once a week. When he asked what was behind my desire for counseling, it caught me off guard. I hadn't thought that far into it. I actually thought about making something up. But I just admitted, "I don't know why I want to meet with you, man. I'm not sure how this even works." I listed a few reasons that didn't apply. "I don't have a problem with pornography," I told him. "I don't hit my wife. I don't have any addictions to drugs. I had a pretty good childhood, as far as I know."

Then I tried to put my need into words. "I just feel like I want to do some work on my interior life so I can be fit to lead the people God has called me to lead. And I just thought I'd see if you did that kind of thing."

He said, "Nobody has ever called me for preventive counseling. Usually people call me after their lives have fallen apart."

Pause.

Dang it. I knew this was a dumb idea.

Then he continued. "Actually, Steven, this sounds great. I'm excited to help. Let's set it up."

We did. And what started as a seemingly harebrained impulse turned into a fruitful long-term relationship. I met with Lance almost every Wednesday morning for the next three years. Going into a counselor's office felt a little embarrassing at first. I mean, I'm the pastor of a big church here in town. What if somebody sees me in the counselor's office? They'll think their pastor's crazy.

But you know what? I decided to own it. There's way too much at stake for me to worry about what people might think. I have to keep my edge, no matter what it takes. And a spiritual edge is not something I can fake.

One Sunday I stood up in front of my church and made an announcement. It went something like this: "I want you all to know that I've started seeing a professional Christian counselor. Regularly. You as a church are paying for it. Don't worry. My marriage isn't on the fritz. I'm not burned out or strung out or anything like that. It's just that...well, I want to keep my edge. I want to do this right. I want you to have a healthy pastor, and I want to be a husband and a father and a man who loves God more and more each and every day. So there you have it. Like it or not, your pastor is a little crazy. So are you. We all need help staying on track. And I've decided this is the best way for me to get that help."

The congregation burst into applause.

And what Raymond Culpepper experienced through a trip back to his father's starting place, I experienced through my weekly trips to the counselor's office. In each session with Lance, as I talked through my weaknesses, hang-ups, and tendencies to lose my edge, he gave me tools to stay sharp. He helped me understand how to base my security in my identity in Christ, not in the nauseating ups and downs of church attendance and professional performance. He helped me learn how to process criticism without becoming bitter in my soul or losing my love for people.

Most of all, he helped me see that no matter how much I struggle day to day, I'm never farther from God than a prayer:

"God, help me get back to the place where I belong in You."

> > >

Have I graduated from Ax Head Retrieval Academy? Of course not. Do I still struggle sometimes with losing my edge, my temper, my perspective, my discipline? I do. No amount of counseling will ever fix that completely.

But I've learned that the greater life isn't about living the perfect life. It's about keeping your passion intact, no matter what.

Proverbs 24:16 says,

> Though a righteous man falls seven times, he rises again.

Sometimes it seems as if God has extended that promise to seven hundred thousand times for me. I'm thankful He's the God of another chance.

The next time you lose your momentum in daily life as you're chasing after God's best for you, don't give up and conclude that it's over. The greater life hasn't ended for you. It's only out of sight under the waters of the ordinary. And God can resurface it, supernaturally, as many times as it takes. As many times as you're willing.

Cry out to God. Ask yourself, *Where did it fall?* Then go back to that place, pick it back up, and keep moving forward into the greater things God has for you.

You've come too far to give up now.

Open My Eyes

We've encountered some beautiful and powerful stories from the life of Elisha and in the lives of everyday people. I hope you've been inspired. I hope you're drawing up plans to dream bigger and start smaller.

But at the same time you are determining to ignite God's vision for your life, an enemy is conspiring to kill it before it sees the light of day.

Not just one enemy, actually. It's more like a coalition of forces.

Let's start with people.

The Cast of Characters

All around you are those who are still content with the ordinary. They're wondering why you aren't anymore. You've moved on to greater things, but they're wishing you'd come back. Problem is, since you naturally don't want to pursue your new life alone, you're going to be tempted to rejoin them.

They are the critics and eye rollers who don't mind saying you're crazy to believe that God can use your life in such a great way. The folks who will brazenly tell you that you have no business breaking out of their own well-engineered expectations for you. That negative friend who is constantly pointing out life's limitations rather than God's possibilities. The controlling boss who would rather you keep running like an effective cog in the system than threaten his status quo. The jealous coworker who is trying to undermine you at every turn. The overbearing parents who would rather impress their dreams on you than let you pursue your own.

As a pastor, I'm all too familiar with these kinds of people and their ability to keep you from fulfilling God's dreams for you. I used to be naive about critics. I heard pastors I admired talk about the constant agitation of naysayers, but I didn't take it seriously. I thought that as long as I kept my heart right and my motives pure, people would at least appreciate my desire to serve God and help people. As it turns out—not so much.

In a digital age in which we have unlimited access to an unlimited variety of opinions, not every opinion is worth listening to. Just the other night I randomly checked my Twitter feed and found a guy who attributed a preposterous quote to me. Something about how I didn't believe in the importance of discipleship.

Pure slander. I never said that or anything like it.

As much as I would like to say I've learned to smile sweetly and pray, "Help them, Jesus," in those scenarios, I must confess that I wanted to lay hands on him. In the Quentin Tarantino way, not the Bible way. That stuff stings.

As our church has grown, we've had to overcome all sorts of opposition. We've had to deal with negative media pieces and antagonistic, unscrupulous reporters. A local television station once ran a piece suggesting that our church didn't accept people with physical or mental disabilities. This was less than a month after we had released thousands of dollars and commissioned hundreds of hours of volunteer efforts to support a local organization that ministers to those with disabilities. Some of the best volunteers we have are people with disabilities. Added to that, my sister-in-law Joy is disabled, and I would punch someone in the mouth to defend her. My mom has given much of her adult life to serving people with disabilities. Why would a reporter suggest that we would *ever* offer anything less than love, support, and compassion to those in a position of such vulnerability?

It was one of those days when I thought about applying for a job selling Les Pauls at Guitar Center. Let somebody else have this ministry gig.

This isn't me having a pity party. I'm well aware that brothers and sisters in other parts of the world are dealing with real, violent persecution. And you may have to deal with sources of negativity that are far greater than mine. I can turn off Twitter or the local news. You can't turn off your boss or your mom, and I wouldn't suggest you try. But my point is, I know how crippling encounters with these kinds of people can be when you're trying to pursue the life God has called you to.

Put Them Out

Maybe the reason some of us feel surrounded by opposition as we try to live for God is that we have surrounded ourselves with the wrong people. They aren't hiding outside our windows waiting to ambush us. They are sitting at our tables by personal invitation.

If you're going to do what God has called you to do, you have to intentionally bring the people into your life He wants you to have. And put out the ones who subtract from your potential.

This isn't just me talking here. Consider:

- Solomon was condemned for surrounding himself with foreign wives who led him into idolatry (see 1 Kings 11:4).
- Paul encourages us to "not be misled: 'Bad company corrupts good character'" (1 Corinthians 15:33).
- Jesus put out the people in Jairus's home who laughed at Him when He wanted to bring Jairus's daughter back to life (see Mark 5:40).

The concept of putting people out of your life may not sound very loving. But I'm not talking about drawing a circle around people and refusing to care for them. I'm talking about drawing a circle around your spirit and allowing only certain people to affect it. There's a big difference.

And it makes a big difference. If you listed the five people who have the most access to your life, I could predict with remarkable accuracy the course your life is going to take. Not because I'm Nostradamus. It's just simple logic. The people who have significant input into your life shape who you'll become and what you'll do.

That was a tough lesson to learn when I started going after God's greater plans for me. One of the first things I did after giving my life to the Lord was to have a little meetup with some of the fellas in my life. They were nice guys. But they weren't interested in pursuing God's greater vision.

So I took them to Taco Bell, my treat. "Some things need to change," I told them. "I still love you. I still want to be your friend. I still want to be there for you. But I can't hang with you and go everywhere you go anymore. Because we're not heading in the same direction."

It was challenging to get those words out. I don't think they fully understood. I'm sure they didn't like it. But I had to accept that if they didn't want God's best for me, I couldn't give them full access to my life. And you know what? I think deep down they respected that.

Don't get me wrong. I'm not saying you need to abandon everybody who isn't going after greater things like you are. That's arrogance and the opposite of the attitude of Jesus, who was a friend of sinners (see Luke 7:34).

And I know you have people in your life—family and co-workers, for example—you can't get rid of. This isn't a license to change your last name or a command to quit your job. You'll just have to approach these relationships in a different way going forward.

The season when you are waking up to the greater call on

your life is a powerful but fragile time. You'll face enough challenges ahead without taking along your own saboteurs. Be careful, intentional, and bold.

>>>

How can you identify the people you need to put out of your life for a season or altogether? I've found it helpful to ask a few pointed questions:

1. Who in my life leads me to attitudes or actions outside of what God prescribes for me in His Word?

2. Who leaves me drained rather than empowered after a typical conversation?

3. Who keeps me thinking smaller rather than helping me dream bigger?

4. Who constantly asserts that what I'm attempting to do for God will not work?

If there are people in your life who fit these descriptions, it might be time to limit their access to you. If that's not possible, brainstorm some creative ways to limit their impact. You won't be unloving to do it. Actually, nothing you can do is more loving for those around you than positioning yourself to be all that God has called you to be. To truly love people means to love God first and foremost.

Of course, it's not just avoiding negative people that positions you for God's best. On the more positive side, you need mentors who are already living in faithful obedience and who are willing to impart their stories and wisdom into your life.

People who have already experienced the opposition but have also seen firsthand the power of God's faithfulness. People who will teach you by example how to recognize God at work in your life. People who can look you eyeball to eyeball when you feel surrounded and remind you:

You're not alone.

God is with you.

And I'm with you too.

Brace for It

Besides negative people, you'll also face an army of distractions and competing ideas, values, interests, and events. Life's daily demands exert a strong downward pull into the tyranny of the ordinary.

Behind it all is the one the Scriptures call the Adversary.

Satan is the maestro of mediocrity. And he will arrange all those competing voices and forces in just the right manner to prevent the truth you've been receiving from settling in. He's conspiring to keep you in your routine, to keep you in front of the television, to keep you stuck in low-level pursuits and relationships. To get you back behind the plow. For good.

The moment you venture outside the safety of this book, you will find yourself surrounded. You're going to feel like a lone island of God-inspired greatness surrounded by a sea of normalcy and complacency. I'm not saying this to scare you. My intention is to prepare you. When you know a hit is coming, you can brace for it.

So what will you do? When you put down this book and it feels as though it's you against the world, how will you keep reaching?

The key to victory is right in front of you—if you open your eyes to see it. The world is against you, yes. But the One who has overcome the world is with you and for you.

That's easy to say but sometimes difficult to see.

Oh, My Lord

In one of the last times we encounter Elisha in the Bible, chaos has once again ensued. The king of Aram has gone to war against Israel. But every time the king of Aram tries to make a strategic move against the people, Israel anticipates it. They don't have undercover spies in Aram's camp; they have something greater—an aging prophet who through the power of God is able to tell the king of Israel every word the king of Aram whispers in his bedroom. Without a single wiretap.

> Time and again Elisha warned the king, so that he was on his guard. (2 Kings 6:10)

When the king of Aram learns that it is Elisha who keeps thwarting his schemes, he becomes enraged and sends soldiers to seize him. Good strategy. Take out Israel's secret weapon, and they're done. So under the cloak of night, an enemy force surrounds Dothan, the city where Elisha is living.

Early the next morning one of Elisha's attendants notices

the Aramean chariots surrounding the city. Seized with fear, he runs to Elisha. "Oh, my lord," the servant cries, "what shall we do?" (verse 15).

You ever had one of those moments? One of those days? One of those shaking seasons of fear and uncertainty? I have.

Pursuing God's purpose can be exhilarating. It can also be terrifying.

If you want to live surrounded by God's miracles, you have to come to terms with the fact that you'll always be surrounded by enemies. You'll often be amazed at what God can do through you. Then again, you'll experience plenty of moments that are more like 2 Kings 6:15. You'll find yourself looking up to heaven, shaking your head in uncertainty, praying:

"Oh, my Lord, what shall I do?"

The opposition can be overwhelming.

But look at what Elisha tells his servant:

Don't be afraid... Those who are with us are more than those who are with them. (verse 16)

Is the old man delusional? The last time I checked, the entire cast of good guys in this situation consists of one old man and an errand boy. They are encircled by an overpowering force bent on killing them. Just as you may be feeling right now, by all accounts the odds are stacked against them.

But right after his puzzling statement, Elisha prays:

O LORD, open his eyes so he may see. (verse 17)

Elisha doesn't pray that God will send down fire as Elijah did on Mount Carmel. And he doesn't pray that God will send a larger army to their rescue. He just prays that the servant will see *what God already has in place.*

In that moment God opens the servant's eyes. He sees "the hills full of horses and chariots of fire all around Elisha" (verse 17).

They are not alone. They never were. They never would be. Heaven's army surrounds the enemy that surrounds them.

Of course, the Arameans don't see what they are up against, so they attack the city. When they do, Elisha asks God to strike them with blindness. (Apparently this supernatural eyesight thing works both ways.)

Then, in one of the most unorthodox and unpredictable moves imaginable, Elisha calls out to the now-blind army before him, "This is not the road and this is not the city. Follow me, and I will lead you to the man you are looking for" (verse 19).

It isn't enough to strike them blind. Elisha has to mess with them. He leads the enemy warriors from Dothan all the way into the city center of Samaria, home of the king of Israel. When the Lord opens their eyes, they see that they are trapped.

Instead of letting Israel destroy the shocked Arameans, Elisha pulls one more surprise. He tells his king to roll out a feast for their enemies and send them on their way.

The biblical historian closes his report with what seems like a wink: "So the bands from Aram stopped raiding Israel's territory" (verse 23).

A Prophetic Perspective

Those who are with us are more than those who are with them…
Open his eyes so he may see.

Those aren't just dead words from the distant past. Or words that were true at one time but not anymore. I believe that, by the power of the Holy Spirit, the words of the prophet Elisha are full of life again, surging through the centuries to speak into your situation. The Word of God that never returns void is hurdling over the distractions and opposition coming at you. It's an optimistic word. A hopeful word. It's a word that takes seriously the reality of the resistance but takes more seriously the reality of the power of the Resurrection inside you. It's a word that is calling you to come up a little higher to see what God sees instead of looking through dirty glasses from your limited perspective.

Those who are with you are more than those who are with them.

You're not alone. Never have been. Never will be.

The Enemy has conspired against you, but God has conspired against him. The Enemy that opposes you could rightly be called great, because he has significant influence and power. But the Word of God says,

> The one who is in you is greater than the one who is in the world. (1 John 4:4)

Don't think of this as a pep talk. Think of it as a prophetic prayer. I'm praying the words of Elisha over you as you near the end of this book: "O Lord, please open their eyes so they may see."

Until now, maybe you've been looking at all the obstacles to your greater life. You've seen the army:

- Of critical people, reminding you of all the ways you've blown it and of all the things you are and all the things you are not.
- Of reasons why this greater life is not practical, not attainable.
- Of weaknesses inside you.
- Of sin tempting you.
- Of past failures marching like foot soldiers over the hope God has stirred inside you.

But are you seeing what God sees? Have you seen your life from His perspective? Your Father sees something *more* than you see…and He wants you to see it too. Even when you don't *know* so, you can rest in the reality that God *says* so.

My Father Says

Even though all three of my kids, Elijah, Graham, and Abbey, are under the age of seven, I talk to them all the time about how special they are. I believe parents have the power to build or destroy confidence in their kids. From the time they were probably too little to understand, I've tried to speak prophetically over my kids. Truths like "You're special." "You're awesome." "You're brilliant." "You're handsome." "You're beautiful."

"You're a leader." "You're a genius." Why leave it to some dumb middle schooler one day to give them his assessment of who they are based on his own juvenile insecurities? I want my children to already know who they are.

A good parenting strategy, if I do say so myself. And it has worked perfectly.

Until recently, when it backfired just a bit.

The other day I heard Elijah and Graham fighting at a pretty normal intensity level, but out of nowhere the dialogue turned interesting. Elijah was trying to boss his younger brother around. Eventually Graham exploded.

"Elijah, you can't tell me what to do *all the time*!"

Elijah's response was an instant classic: "Yes, I can. I'm a *genius*."

Uh-oh.

I wasted no time getting to the bottom of this. "Elijah, did I just hear you tell Graham that you're a genius?"

"Yes sir."

"Why did you tell him that?"

"Because, Daddy, you told me I was."

Touché. A comeback worthy of a genius.

I'm usually quick on my feet. But in this case, all I could come up with was, "Hey, boys, just…stop fighting, okay? Because…just…stop fighting. Or I'm taking away your Legos for, like, a lot of days."

That bought me some time. But now I had a dilemma. I needed to find a way to reinforce to my kid that, yes, he is special. But I also know it isn't in his best interest to walk around thinking he is perfect—and telling everyone about it. There's a fine line between confidence and Kanye.

I was at a loss until one night I suddenly had a parenting breakthrough. I called Elijah into my bedroom and told him to get under the covers and put his head on my chest. Then I reviewed the events from a few days earlier.

"Buddy," I said gently, "you can't go around telling people you're a genius all the time. That's not good. It's going to make people think you think you're better than they are. You see what I'm saying?"

"Yes sir."

"And that's not good, is it?"

"No sir."

"All right. So I've got a plan. From now on, this is what I want you to do. When someone asks you something like 'Are you a genius?' I want you to look right back at them and say this: 'My daddy says I am.'

"Or, if somebody asks you, 'Hey, Elijah, are you handsome?' tell them, 'My daddy says I am.'

"See, when you put it that way, it doesn't have so much to do with *you*. It has more to do with how your *father* sees you. Does this make sense?"

His head nodded on my chest. "It does," he said.

He got it.

These days I quiz him all the time. It's our little thing now, like a secret handshake.

"Hey, Elijah, are you awesome?"

He doesn't blink. "My daddy says I am."

"Are you amazing?"

With a little more swagger now: "My daddy says I am."

"Are you the most wonderful little boy on the planet?"

Bursting with confidence: "My daddy says I am!"

Some of the most humbling lessons I've learned about my relationship with God have come through little parenting incidents like this. Just as I'm preparing my sons for the war zone called middle school, God is preparing His children for the opposition we face every day. Either way, the lesson is the same. What matters most is not what I think I am or am not. Or what others think I am or am not.

What matters is what my Father sees in me and what He says about me.

But I wonder if most Christians even know what their Father has said about them. Who He says they are. What He sees in them. What He believes they're capable of conquering through His power and grace.

My guess is, probably not. Maybe that's why so many Christians walk around in perpetual defeat.

God's Power, Your Strength

Do you ever feel as if you bounce from one weak moment to another? Life is clicking right along, you're gaining courage and momentum, then your kid comes home from school with a note from the principal's office. Or you think you'll finally start gaining ground on your debt until an unexpected trip to the ER cuts your progress off at the knees. Or you finally think you've found the one relationship you've been dreaming of your whole life, and that person suddenly gets cold feet or a wandering eye, and all those dreams shatter.

And you stare at the reflection of yourself in the mirror, and you see weakness. Loss. Rejection.

What you don't see is power.

How can we miss it—when our God has all the power in the world? It's because we have to look at our situations with more than just human insight. Often we have to see, discern, and realize God's power not with a physical sense but with a deeper awareness. Scripture calls that sense *the eyes of our hearts.*

Ephesians 1:18–21 contains some of the greatest truths in the entire Bible about what God sees and says about us. Paul's sentences radiate so much power; I want you to consider them word by word:

> I pray also that the eyes of your heart may be enlight-
> ened in order that you may know the hope to which he
> has called you, the riches of his glorious inheritance in
> the saints, and his incomparably great power for us who
> believe. That power is like the working of his mighty
> strength, which he exerted in Christ when he raised
> him from the dead and seated him at his right hand in
> the heavenly realms, far above all rule and authority,
> power and dominion, and every title that can be given,
> not only in the present age but also in the one to come.

Paul's prayer for the church echoes the prayer of Elisha for his servant: *Open their eyes...* He prays that the Ephesians would know how the power of God is accessible and available to them as ordinary, average, common believers. People like me. People like you.

Paul's prayer is not that Christians might know how powerful *God* is. Nor does he pray that God would *be* powerful, because He already is. Paul doesn't even pray that *we* would have *more* power, because in Christ we already have all the power we need for anything we are facing in our lives. Any circumstance. Every form of opposition we're going to encounter.

Instead he prays that we would *know* "that power...which he exerted in Christ" for ourselves—and that this power would become a mighty strength in our lives.

Why does Paul pray this way? Because he knows the truth: *It is possible for God to have all the power and yet for His people to live in total weakness.*

God isn't short on power. Power belongs to God. He has it all. Jesus said, "All authority in heaven and on earth has been given to me" (Matthew 28:18). But God's power within you is only potential until you convert it into strength—by faith and action.

Living in strength is all about taking hold of God's power and exerting it in our lives. But we can't put it to use if we don't know it's there. And we can't live it out if it's always overshadowed by reminders of our weaknesses.

So when the devil or any of the voices in his choir start bombarding you with messages about your weakness, recall the powerful truths your Father says about you in Ephesians 1 and countless other places throughout the Bible. Look back at your adversary, and make the statement of affirmation my son has learned so well: "My Father says I am."

Do you really think you're capable of fulfilling what God has called you to do?

"My Father says I am. I don't know how I'm going to do it, but the power of the Resurrection is in me. I don't feel capable. But my Father says I am."

Do you really think you're going to make it through this trial?

"My Father says I am."

Do you really think you're going to overcome this temptation?

"My Father says I am."

Do you really think you're capable of living the greater life?

"Honestly, no. But God is in me, and He is greater, and all things are possible with my God. My Father says I'm able."

My Father says I am.

We don't live by what our physical eyes see. We live by what God sees and by what He says. When I live by what He says, He opens my eyes to see what He sees. And He sees infinite power and potential in me. And in you.

It doesn't matter how strong *they* are; what matters is how strong *He* is *in* you.

Open your eyes.

You're not alone.

Not Alone

Since the same Holy Spirit that once rested only on special prophets like Elisha has now been poured out on all flesh, you don't have to be a prophet to see your life as God sees it.

So I want you to take a moment and pray the prayer of Elisha for yourself in the first person:

"O Lord, open my eyes that I may see."

You may want to pray that a few more times. Pray until God allows you to glimpse something of His perspective on your life: that while you are surrounded by great opposition, you are empowered by a greater God. God's glory and power are all around you and within you. The greater life has already been laid out for you.

Step out in His mighty strength. You don't have to deliberate, agonize, or theorize. Recall the truth of what your Father says about you. Strip the mechanisms of hurt and disobedience that have constrained you. And do exactly what He's calling you to do.

Close your eyes and pray.

Open your eyes and see.

Then take up your cross and follow.

You're not alone.

Strike the Water

Think back with me to Elisha's years of training with Elijah. The years after his life behind the plow, the years before his remarkably greater life as prophet to the nation of Israel.

Look back with me at the moment when he crossed over from old to new, from routine to remarkable, from ox driver to wonder-worker...

You know the story now:

Elijah had been the one who tapped into Elisha's potential and threw the cloak of his real destiny around the plowman's shoulders. Then, together, senior prophet and junior prophet had walked away from the field of Elisha's former life—Elijah into many more years of spectacular miracles in the courts of kings, but Elisha into temporary obscurity.

We don't know exactly what happened during those years. The Bible offers only one line about Elisha's story during that season:

[Elisha] set out to follow Elijah and became his attendant. (1 Kings 19:21)

We don't know exactly how the relationship between these two men developed, either. Maybe it started simply as one of prophetic professionals. Maybe it was more like father and son from the very beginning. Either way, I can imagine that Elisha watched dumbstruck as Elijah performed miracles and went mano a mano with false prophets and tyrant kings.

Then one day God raised the stakes for Elisha.

For each of us there comes a time when we can't just live out of the abundance of faith instilled in the great men and women who have gone before us. We have to walk in faith for ourselves. We have our own work. We have our own gifts.

We have our own step of faith to take.

And so finally the day came when God loved Elisha by taking the training wheels off his bike...

> > >

Elijah and Elisha are walking toward their home base in Gilgal when Elijah tells his protégé he must go on to Bethel—alone. But Elisha will hear nothing of it: "As surely as the LORD lives and as you live, I will not leave you" (2 Kings 2:2).

So together they go down to Bethel, where the company of prophets comes out to meet Elisha. Skipping the small talk, they ask him, "Do you know that the LORD is going to take your master from you today?" (verse 3).

Unwilling to contemplate losing his spiritual father, Elisha cuts them off. "Yes, I know," he says, "but do not speak of it."

Elijah again attempts to go on ahead of his heartbroken

spiritual son. "Stay here, Elisha," he says. "The LORD has sent me to Jericho" (verse 4).

Again Elisha refuses: "As surely as the LORD lives and as you live, I will not leave you."

And they walk on together to Jericho. Like a vinyl record skipping, the moment when the prophets greeted Elisha in Bethel is replayed there with eerie precision. "Do you know that the LORD is going to take your master from you today?" the local prophets ask (verse 5). Again, Elisha will hear none of it.

One more time Elijah attempts to press on without his protégé. "Stay here; the LORD has sent me to the Jordan" (verse 6).

One last time Elisha replies, "As surely the LORD lives and as you live, I will not leave you." So together they travel on to the Jordan.

Beside the river, the old man and the younger man stare across the expanse of water in front of them and the even vaster expanse of destiny the water represents. Behind them and some distance away, fifty prophets have followed to see what will happen next.

Elijah takes his cloak, rolls it up, lifts it high above his head, and then with all his might brings it down in an arc to strike the water. This act brings together into one story the God of Joshua at the Jordan so many years before and the God of Elijah in the here and now.

Strike.

The water parts, and the two men cross on dry ground.

None of the witnesses that day misses the immensity of the moment—Israel's glory days are no longer behind them. The God who showed Himself so powerful for Joshua is showing Himself just as powerfully for Elijah.

Will he do the same, they must have wondered, *for Elisha?*

Perhaps only moments later Elijah is taken up to heaven. The Bible describes the historic event like this:

> As they were walking along and talking together, suddenly a chariot of fire and horses of fire appeared and separated the two of them, and Elijah went up to heaven in a whirlwind. Elisha saw this and cried out, "My father! My father! The chariots and horsemen of Israel!" And Elisha saw him no more. (verses 11–12)

Elisha tears his own clothes to express his grief. Then he picks up the cloak that had fallen from Elijah and walks back to the edge of the river. On the other side, the company of prophets are still lined up on the shore, waiting and watching.

Who is this Elisha now? Is he still a student and servant of someone greater, or has he now become greater himself by God's anointing?

They wait and watch.

Elisha lifts the cloak high above his head, and then with all his might brings it down in an arc...

Strike.

"When he struck the water," the Bible says, "it divided to the right and to the left, and [Elisha] crossed over" (verse 14).

After that moment, history would be rewritten—Elisha's history and that of everyone who came into contact with him. God would indeed show Himself just as strongly for Elisha. This prophet would, in fact, go on to do twice as many miracles as his mentor. And the events of his ministry years—those amazing things we've looked at together in this book—would be celebrated like those of Joshua.

If Elisha's story already had a sense of destiny, now it has a sense of inevitability. When the cloak strikes the water, there is no going back.

The burned plows behind him. His long apprenticeship completed. God's greater calling ahead of him.

Strike.

The Mantle Is Yours

And so comes the end of the book that is actually a beginning.

Right now you are in the same place Elisha was on that historic day by the river. You are standing at the crossing point to your future. You don't have a school of prophets watching from a distance. More likely for you, standing at some distance is your very own cast of parents, friends, aunts and uncles, coworkers and spectators, maybe a spouse, maybe your children—all waiting for you to take your place. They are waiting for you to do the things only you can do by the power of God's Spirit. They are waiting for God to touch them through you, even if they don't know it yet.

Can you feel the weight of this moment? The moment when God's past faithfulness intersects with your present? When ancient history becomes the story of your life?

Elijah passed on his mantle to Elisha. Through your surrender to God's Spirit, the mantle of Elisha has been passed on to you. Think of the scriptures you've encountered in this book as your cloak. Bound up in God's Word is the impartation you need to leave your life of *good enough* behind and step into the greater life God has had in mind for you all along. You're about to make your crossing. Your divine destiny waits for you on the other side.

You might feel suddenly overwhelmed by a thousand reasons for why it might not work, should not work, and will not work. With the water stretching away in front of you, those thoughts make perfect sense.

But it's time to step out.

This is not a test to see if you are a strong swimmer. This is an invitation to do what God has asked of you so He can then show you what He can do.

Take the cloak. Take the word God has spoken to you. Roll it up. This anointing—this presence of God, this boldness and authority that come from God's Spirit alone—is for you.

Don't test the water. Don't tap the water. Don't put your toe in the water.

Strike the water.

And see the world as you've known it split. See the impossible become possible. Bear witness to a work of God in you that will leave the world breathless. The water is deep, but it is nothing compared to the power of the word that God has birthed inside you.

You didn't pick this book up by accident. The hand of God is on you right here, right now, and this is your moment. We've looked at inspiring stories from Elisha and others who have set out to pursue their greater calling. The guarantee for you is the same: whenever you do what God has called you to do—in any situation, in any given moment—He will do something greater.

This is not a moment to look back over your shoulder and replay the comfortable monotony of life behind the plow. This is not a moment to second-guess your capacity to hear from God. All the stories and miracle narratives have been leading up to this moment, pregnant with sacred expectation. God Himself has been plotting to bring you to this moment, when the faith of Elisha would become your own and finally be embodied in your real life.

> > >

And now, as you step toward the river, I want to pray for you.

I don't presume to know your exact situation or precisely what's waiting for you on the other side of the river. But I have been where you're standing right now. And so, as a person who isn't a master of the greater life but who does know some of what's ahead for you, I pray this for you:

I pray that you will strike the water…where you live.

I pray that you will no longer settle for good enough in your closest relationships, existing together but not really engaging each other. I pray that where you may have settled into patterns of comfort, busyness, and mundane living, you will exchange all that for a greater dream of seeing the glory of God displayed where you live. I pray that the monotonous drone that can come with living together as a family will be replaced by the passionate cadence of a family that follows God together. I pray that you won't settle for raising good boys and girls who don't get on your nerves or interfere with your dreams but who are world changers that chase after God's dream for them.

I pray that you will strike the water…where you work.

I pray that you will never settle for the "good enough" of killing time and drawing a paycheck. Clocking in and clocking out. If God is calling you to step into something new, I pray that He will give you the faith to do so. If God is calling you to step up in the job you already have, I pray that He will give you the passion to do so. Either way, I pray that you will step into the greater life of influence that God has called you to within your work. I pray that your profession will turn into your pulpit, your sport coat become your cloak, your office become a sanctuary, your work become your worship. I pray that, instead of fantasizing about somebody else's life, you will pursue God's greater life for you.

I pray for every young person that you will strike the water…even in your youth and inexperience.

I pray that you won't just be a part of the crowd but that you will begin to lead it. I pray that the people who have been influencing you to a lesser life will be changed by the influence of the greater life you are stepping into. I pray that every voice that has labeled you as anything other than a beloved son or beloved daughter will be silenced and that you will believe only what your Father God has said about you.

Above all, I pray that you will strike the water…in your walk with God.

I pray that you will not be satisfied with living on the fumes of what God did in your life yesterday but that every day will be a new chance to encounter God in a fresh way. I pray you will realize that your relationship with God is only as strong as your most recent encounter with Him. I pray that you won't be content with hearing about how others have walked with God powerfully but that you will walk powerfully with Him yourself.

> > >

For everybody who is sick of playing it safe, for every dreamer who has been devastated and disillusioned, for every undiscovered Elisha determined to show a watching world the greater things our God is capable of…your moment is now. The mantle is yours. Nothing is impossible.

Dream bigger. Start smaller. Ignite God's vision for your life.

Strike.

These Bones

Even prophets get old. Even prophets get sick and die.

Many years after taking up Elijah's mantle of ministry, Elisha is lying on his deathbed. And he is still prophesying—one last time to King Josiah over Israel's future. He is still shaping the rise and fall of nations.

What a life.

But his death itself is a fairly undramatic affair. "Elisha died and was buried" (2 Kings 13:20).

After such a historic life, that's the whole news clip?

Elisha, the anonymous plowman, did even greater miracles than Elijah, Israel's most famous prophet—greater in number and intensity. But no matter how great any of us are in life, we are all buried just the same. Dirt seems to be the great equalizer.

And with that, the story of Elisha is over.

Except it's not.

A few months later a band of Moabites come to invade Israel. As a man is being buried on the same plot of land where

Elisha was laid to rest, the marauding band comes over the horizon. Frightened, the gravediggers hastily throw the dead man into the grave of Elisha.

The elements are no respecter of great men. The once chiseled, robust young man who ran a team of oxen with such vitality has no more muscles or flesh or eyes. Time and desert heat and dry air have reduced the body of Elisha to bones.

The body of the newly deceased man, abandoned like a child's toy, plops clumsily onto the bones of Elisha. And when his cold flesh brushes up against the prophet's brittle bones, color floods back into his cheeks. Breath fills his lungs. The man wakes up in Elisha's grave—and stands to his feet (see verse 21).

Thus began a new life for this unnamed man. A new life that, I think it's safe to assume, was greater.

> > >

Discussion Questions

Because greater happens together…

Chapter 1: Steve and Me

Most believers aren't in imminent danger of ruining their lives. They're facing a danger that's far greater: wasting them.

1. Tell about a time when you found yourself wishing you were accomplishing more in life that really matters. What caused your discontent?

2. As you think back over your Christian life, what has been your most grandiose (and unachievable) pipe dream about doing something great for God?

3. Steven says, "We wake up one day to find ourselves stuck in miserable mediocrity." Is that true for your life right now? If so, describe how you're stuck in mediocrity.

4. What's your reaction to this book's concept of *greater* (as opposed to grandiose *greatness* and mediocre *good enough*)? How does it affect your perspective on your future?

5. If you already have an idea of what greater thing God might have in mind for you, what is it?

Start small: As a group, decide that you're going to be there for each other in your pursuit of greater. Begin by praying for one another, asking God to open your eyes to the greater things He has in store for each of you.

Chapter 2: Lesser Loser Life

In spite of all the parts of us that are anything but good, God is holding the door open to a life that is greater.

1. Describe your own "lesser loser life"—the ways that things like fear, self-doubt, and self-criticism make you question whether you're a candidate for a greater life.

2. If you're troubled by condemning messages in your head, where do you think they come from? (The devil? Memories of other people's words? Your own self-image? Something else?)

3. In the past how has your lesser loser life kept you from doing something you believed God was calling you to do? What do you think that you—and others—might have missed out on as a result?

4. To you, who is a good example of a person who got past his or her lesser loser life to take hold of God's greater things? What can we learn from this example?

5. Steven says, "God doesn't do greater things exclusively through great people. He does them through anyone who is willing to trust Him in greater ways." How would you describe your level of trust in God's ability to do great things through you?

Start small: Taking each person in the group in turn, let everyone else encourage this person by saying why they are confident God can use him or her for greater things. For homework, read Elisha's story in 1 Kings 19:19–21; 2 Kings 2:1–9:13; 13:14–21.

Chapter 3: Dragging Behind

God communicates vision differently to everyone He calls. He is working behind the scenes, orchestrating His destiny for you.

1. How has your life sunk to the level of baseline living, of merely *good enough,* in your relationship with God? In your work or other daily routines? In your close relationships?

2. What evidence have you seen that God is still present and aware of what's going on in your life despite the ways you've been stuck in baseline living?

3. Elisha was once just a guy plowing a field, yet at that very time God was planning to use him. What signs have you seen that God might be working behind the scenes of your life, orchestrating events to set you up for something greater?

4. Lately has God been calling you to something greater? If so, what is that call, and how has it come to you? (If you *haven't* heard God call you lately, give an example of a time when you heard Him call you in the past.)

5. Steven says, "You don't have to get all wrapped up in figuring out *how* God's calling will come to you. Just be ready to respond in faith when it does." What lessons have you learned about being ready to respond to God in faith?

Start small: Maybe one or more people in your group think they are hearing God calling them to something greater but aren't sure. Let these people share; then as a group pray for them and try to help them figure out God's will for their next step.

Chapter 4: Burn the Plows

When God is speaking, one word is more than enough. He's more interested in your full obedience than your total understanding.

1. Steven says if you're going to have a greater life, you have to "burn your plow"—make a decisive break with whatever is keeping you stuck in your old life. What plow is God calling you to burn?

2. What are your fears about burning your plows? What does it make you wonder about the future?

3. What do you see as the plus side of going on a trust journey with God, learning just enough today to take a faith step toward where He wants you to be tomorrow?

4. Sometimes it helps to have a symbolic sign or ceremony of the change you're making, just as Elisha burned his plow and Steven burned his CD collection. What sign or ceremony would help you mark the change you want to make in your life?

5. What might you *lose* if you *don't* burn your plow? What might you *gain* if you *do*?

Start small: How can the members of your group participate in one another's plow-burning ceremonies?

Chapter 5: Digging Ditches

God will often launch a vision that is larger than life by bringing you to a starting point that is small and seemingly insignificant.

1. Which has been a bigger problem in preventing you from experiencing a greater life—not thinking big enough or not starting small enough? Explain.

2. What small steps and practical preparations is God asking you to make for the greater life He wants you to live? In other words, what ditches is He asking you to dig? (They might be actions you take, words you say, prayers you pray, even thoughts you think.)

3. Have you already dug any of those ditches? If so, what were they, and how did it go? If not, what's stopping you?

4. What do your actions (or lack thereof) in starting small say about your faith in God?

5. The ditches we dig are to make room for the rain God will send. What kind of new blessing do you think God wants you to make room for in your life?

Start small: Have everybody state at least one ditch they're going to dig to prepare for greater things to come. Check on each other, and hold each other accountable for getting it done.

Chapter 6: A Little Oil

Stop waiting for what you want, and start working what you've got. Your greatest limitation is God's greatest opportunity.

1. Steven says the greater life doesn't always mean making heroic sacrifices or doing something that impresses others. He says it might mean setting out for mission fields or it might mean staying right where we are. Whatever God calls us to is *greater* for us. What's your reaction to this way of looking at it?

2. Have you been wasting time thinking that if you only had _____, you could serve God better? If so, what's the _____ you've been dwelling on?

3. What do you think it will take for you to give up that kind of fruitless thinking?

4. What is your "widow's oil"? In other words, what are some things you have (gifts, skills, relationships, knowledge, whatever) that God can use in a greater way?

5. How can you put these things to work now for God's greater purposes?

Start small: Spend some time in prayer for God to help everyone in the group start making real progress toward whatever greater goal He has for them.

Chapter 7: Wasted Faith

The journey toward greater things is marked with setbacks and real suffering. But God has never wasted an ounce of your faith.

1. When the Shunammite woman's son died, it must have seemed a contradiction of God's promise to her. In your pursuit of greater, how have you encountered setbacks, tragedy, or even the death of your hopes and dreams? (If you haven't had problems like these lately, think about a time in the past.)

2. What were your feelings when this happened? How did you react?

3. Did you sense the presence of God grieving alongside you? If so, describe that and what it meant to you.

4. What kinds of faith struggles and questions do you have when things go terribly wrong in the midst of pursuing what you think God wants you to do?

5. If you've ever felt that your faith was wasted, tell about that.

Start small: If one or more people in the group are currently grieving setbacks or tragedies, the rest of you can ask how you might be able to help.

Chapter 8: Trust Fund Baby

In God's economy, our greatest setbacks in life can be the greatest setups to seeing God's glory in places we didn't even know to look.

1. Steven puts forward the provocative idea that God has a trust fund for each of us in which He deposits our faith for payouts to come later in ways we do not anticipate. Thus our faith is never really wasted. What is your reaction to this idea?

2. What effect does this concept of the trust fund have on your attitude toward the setbacks and tragedies— all the seemingly unanswered prayers—you've had along the way?

3. What have been some of the most memorable times you've experienced God's blessing or goodness in ways you never expected?

4. Right now, what disappointing situation in your life seems dead and has you feeling defeated? How much trust do you have that Jesus can bring life out of it anyway, just as He brought the Shunammite woman's son back to life?

5. Steven says the key to having faith while we are waiting for God to act is to draw near to Him and focus on His faithfulness. How are you doing this? (It could be by worshiping God, memorizing Scripture, praying with a friend, praising God, or something else.)

Start small: How can the members of your group be resources for each other in drawing nearer to God?

Chapter 9: Saving Captain Awesomesauce

It's possible to have all the external signs of greatness and yet internally yearn for something greater.

1. How has pride shown itself in your life?

2. How has your pride interfered with your attempts to serve God?

3. "There comes a time in the life of every follower of Jesus," Steven says, "when God asks us to do something that will deliver a deathblow to our pride." Has this time come in your life yet? If so, tell about it.

4. Thinking back to the Bible story of Naaman, who balked at the idea of washing in the Jordan River, what is the Jordan River in your life? In other words, what is the one thing about which you would say, "I would do anything God asked me to do—as long as it is not that"?

5. Steven offers two tips for becoming a humble servant of God: obeying immediately when He instructs us to do so, and keeping ourselves small in our relationships. What are some specific ways you can apply these two tips?

Start small: If anyone in the group is at the point of needing to do something humbling in order to prepare for the greater life, let him or her share it with the others and receive their advice or encouragement.

Chapter 10: Where Did It Fall?

Greater isn't an automatic, permanent position; it's an intentional daily decision.

1. Like Elisha's student, have you ever lost your cutting edge—your spiritual momentum—and begun to backslide into the realm of the ordinary? (Maybe you're there right now.) How did you realize what was happening?

2. How did you react when you lost your edge? Did it discourage you? How did this situation affect your life in Christ?

3. Steven says, "No detail or circumstance in my life falls outside [God's] concern.... And since most of our spiritual momentum is gained or lost in the everyday affairs of life, it's good to know that God is actively involved in them." How have you sensed God's presence when you've struggled with losing your edge?

4. According to Steven, if we're feeling spiritually dull, we shouldn't just try harder; we should cry out to God. Can you share a story of a time when trying harder to recover your spiritual passion didn't work? Or when going to God proved to be the turning point instead?

5. If you're stuck in spiritual dullness right now, where did you get off track? How can you go back to that point and recover your passion?

Start small: Get together in groups of two or three, and pray for each other to find a renewed passion and determination to serve God in greater ways.

Chapter 11: Open My Eyes

What matters most is not what you think you are or are not. What matters is what your Father sees in you and what He says about you.

1. Which five people have the most access to your life? Name them. How is each one *encouraging* you in your attempts to live greater for God or *discouraging* you?

2. What can you do to prevent the critics, the eye rollers, and the wet blankets from hindering your progress toward where God wants you to be?

3. Steven says that in addition to negative people, "an army of distractions and competing ideas, values, interests, and events" can also "exert a strong downward pull into the tyranny of the ordinary." What does that army look like for you? How effective have these competing voices been in keeping you stuck in low-level pursuits and relationships?

4. Elisha prayed that God would open the eyes of a companion to see the army of heaven. Would you say

that the eyes of your heart are open to seeing God's almighty power? Why or why not?

5. What would be different in your life if you were living as if you really believed that you have infinite power and potential because of God's being within you? How would you *think* differently? What would you *do* differently?

Start small: Share favorite Bible verses that reveal God's ability to do great things through us despite our own weaknesses.

Chapter 12: Strike the Water

For everybody who is sick of playing it safe, for every dreamer who has been disillusioned, your moment is now. The mantle is yours.

1. When Elisha struck the Jordan River with his cloak, that was the sign he was ready to step into the future as a prophet in his own right. What does it mean for you to strike the water and move into the greater future God has planned for you? Identify your decisive next step.

2. How do you feel about going for greater in your life? Are you ready? What are you excited about?

3. How do you think your greater life will affect your family and close relationships? Your work, schooling, or other everyday routine? Your spiritual life?

4. What do you hope to see God accomplish through you?

5. How can the others in the group pray for you and support you?

Start small: Ask God to ignite His vision in a way that will burn for the rest of your lives. Praise Him for what He will do!

Acknowledgments

THE NAMES	THE NICKNAMES
Holly	The Angel of This House
Elijah, Graham, and Abbey	Pajama-Bottom Band
Bracy Train	Midlife City Slickers
Murrill and Deborah	Estrogen Inc.
Chunks and Amy Corbett	Royal Beasts
Inner Circle	Ring Bearers
Elevation Staff	Heart and Soul
Elevation Creative	Jagged Little Pills
Elevation Worship	Wolves Like Us
Eric and Nicole Phillips	OXEN!
Pastor Craig Groeschel	Technobishop of the World, My Hero
Jonathan Martin	Fiery Wildman Mentor/ BBPBear
Lysa TerKeurst	Sweet Subconscious Genius Friend
Tom Winters	The Good Lord's Agent
David Kopp	My Bob Rock

The Team at WaterBrook
    Multnomah

Paul Cunningham

Eric Stanford

The Elevation Nation

Regulators

Marco...

Brother Bottomline

Greater Things...

About the Author

STEVEN FURTICK, author of the best-selling *Sun Stand Still,* is founder and lead pastor of Elevation Church, which in only six years has grown to more than ten thousand in regular attendance at six locations. He holds a master of divinity degree from Southern Baptist Theological Seminary. He and his wife, Holly, have three children: Elijah, Graham, and Abbey. They make their home near Charlotte, North Carolina.

DREAM **BIGGER.** START **SMALLER.**
TAKE THE GREATER MESSAGE TO YOUR GROUP

Now that you've discovered a *greater* way, you can take it even further with the **GREATER DVD & PARTICIPANT'S GUIDE**. In four sessions, you and your small group, church or business team will learn to apply the key principles of **GREATER**.

>>>

THE GREATER DVD & PARTICIPANT'S GUIDE EXPERIENCE

- An Intro Video and Four Teaching Sessions by Steven Furtick
- A Study Guide created to compliment the DVD teachings
- Original Worship Song for each session, written and performed by Elevation Worship to facilitate a time of reflection

Recorded on location in London and Israel.

For a sample of the
GREATER DVD & PARTICIPANT'S GUIDE visit
WWW.GREATERBOOK.COM

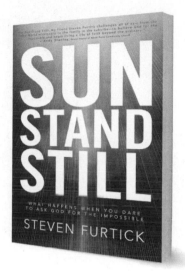

WHAT HAPPENS WHEN YOU DARE TO ASK GOD FOR THE IMPOSSIBLE

If the size of your vision for your life isn't intimidating to you, there's a good chance it is insulting to God.

In his first book, Pastor Steven Furtick challenges you to walk in audacious faith and watch God do the impossible in your life. No dream is too big when God is involved, and there is unlimited potential in the life of every believer through Jesus. Steven shows that faith is the most vital building block in your relationship with God as you live out what He has put in your heart.

IN SUN STAND STILL, YOU WILL DISCOVER HOW TO:

Reconnect with your God-sized purpose and potential

Believe in the promises of God even in uncertainty

Activate your faith through hearing, speaking, and doing the Word of God

Pray with urgency, boldness, and expectancy

Start a movement in your life, your church and your community

FIND OUT MORE ABOUT THE MOVEMENT AT WWW.SUNSTANDSTILL.ORG

GREATER is much more than a book. It is an immersive experience. The new album from Elevation Worship, **NOTHING IS WASTED**, is designed to follow the narrative of **GREATER**. The 12 original songs written by the worship team at Elevation Church correspond with the chapters of the book.

SONGS INCLUDE:

Great In Us

Let Go

In Your Presence

I Have Decided

We're Not Alone

I Will Trust In You

Unchanging God

Nothing Is Wasted

Be Lifted High

Lift Us Out

Open Up Our Eyes

Greater

FOR MORE INFORMATION, VISIT:

WWW.ELEVATIONWORSHIP.COM